CLASSIC CAMARO

Restoration, Repair & Upgrades

Previously published as *Camaro Owner's Handbook*

Ron Sessions

HPBooks

HPBooks

Published by the Penguin Group

Penguin Group (USA) Inc.

375 Hudson Street, New York, New York 10014, USA

Penguin Group (Canada), 90 Eglinton Avenue East, Suite 700, Toronto, Ontario M4P 2Y3, Canada
(a division of Pearson Penguin Canada Inc.)
Penguin Books Ltd., 80 Strand, London WC2R 0RL, England
Penguin Group Ireland, 25 St. Stephen's Green, Dublin 2, Ireland (a division of Penguin Books Ltd.)
Penguin Group (Australia), 250 Camberwell Road, Camberwell, Victoria 3124, Australia
(a division of Pearson Australia Group Pty. Ltd.)
Penguin Books India Pvt. Ltd., 11 Community Centre, Panchsheel Park, New Delhi—110 017, India
Penguin Group (NZ), 67 Apollo Drive, Rosedale, Auckland 0632, New Zealand
(a division of Pearson New Zealand Ltd.)
Penguin Books (South Africa) (Pty.) Ltd., 24 Sturdee Avenue, Rosebank, Johannesburg 2196, South Africa

Penguin Books Ltd., Registered Offices: 80 Strand, London WC2R 0RL, England

While the author has made every effort to provide accurate telephone numbers and Internet addresses at the time of publication, neither the publisher nor the author assumes any responsibility for errors, or for changes that occur after publication. Further, the publisher does not have any control over and does not assume any responsibility for author or third-party websites or their content.

Originally published in a different form as *Camaro Owner's Handbook*.

CLASSIC CAMARO

PRINTING HISTORY
First HPBooks edition / April 1999
Revised HPBooks edition / May 2011

ISBN: 978-1-55788-564-7

PRINTED IN THE UNITED STATES OF AMERICA
10 9 8 7 6 5 4 3 2 1

NOTICE: The information in this book is true and complete to the best of our knowledge. All recommendations on parts and procedures are made without any guarantees on the part of the author or the publisher. Tampering with, altering, modifying, or removing any emissions-control device is a violation of federal law. Author and publisher disclaim all liability incurred in connection with the use of this information. We recognize that some words, engine names, model names, and designations mentioned in this book are the property of the trademark holder and are used for identification purposes only. This is not an official publication.

C O N T E N T S

ACKNOWLEDGMENTS

When you think about it, none of us would have Chevrolet's fetching sport coupe to drive and enjoy, let alone restore and write books about, if it were not for the many talented and dedicated men and women at General Motors who designed, engineered and developed the first-generation Camaros more than forty years ago. Though sales numbers rose and fell with economic swings over the decades, and there were some scary times in the early part of this century when we thought the Camaro might be gone for good, the bright minds at Chevrolet managed to keep the Camaro candle lit. Those GM employees involved with the original car have long since retired and some may have made their last cruise run, but now there is a new crew hard at work making today's fifth-generation Camaro everything it can be.

There's no denying that the Camaro delivers an unforgettable driving experience. Evolved over a half century, the American muscle car distills a unique blend of sporty style, sharp handling, V-8 performance and rear-drive fun, and it does so at prices the average joe can afford. It's a tip of the hat to the youth of the American middle class, or folks who just want to feel that way.

In the course of gathering the information for this book, I snapped thousands of photos, made hundreds of phone calls, wrote countless e-mails, and filled dozens of notepads with grease-stained scribbles and tips. But

Classic Camaro: Restoration, Repair & Upgrades would never have come about if it were not for the reams of information and generous help provided by Camaro restoration experts and aftermarket parts suppliers.

First and foremost, a thanks to Tom Monroe for putting me on the career path editing and writing HPBooks how-to automotive books; Michael Lutfy for the encouragement to tackle this assignment; and Jeff Leonard and Bob Brennan of Classic Industries for the parts horsepower to get many a Camaro project underway.

Around the Sessions family's neighborhood, Marty Foltz added his contagious ebullience on first-generation cars, uncanny knack for sniffing out unconventional sources for original parts, and willingness to give up precious weekend hours turning wrenches on Camaros for the camera. Larry McNeill took the time to explain the ins and outs of Rally Sport hideaway headlamps. And Larry Wright snaked wires to unreachable places.

Also, a special thanks to Stewart Haslam of Year One, Inc., John Sloan and Curt Strohaker of the Eastwood Company, Bob Baum of Baum's Auto Supply in Mission Viejo, California, the folks at Custom Autosound and especially the late Bob Moore of D&R Classic Automotive.

DEDICATION

I'd like to dedicate *Classic Camaro* to the late HPBooks founder, "California" Bill Fisher, who channeled a youthful zest for souping up inline GMC six-cylinder engines into a successful and respected publishing company.

I don't know about you, but one of my pet peeves is dealing with vague repair or assembly instructions. We've all been there at one time or another, screwdriver in one hand, wrench in another the night before a kid's birthday, trying to decipher oddly translated words and cartoonish drawings to assemble that shiny new bicycle. If only they had told me I had to install washer F before nut B…you get my drift. The way I see it, the do-it-yourselfer has to endure way too much trial and error and often suffer costly and time-consuming mistakes to get the job done.

You are in the car hobby at least partly because you enjoy poking around and tinkering with things mechanical. Working with your hands is great therapy, especially if you are like the legions of car enthusiasts out there with a day job that involves sitting at a desk or pounding keys on a computer. But where to go for guidance? Factory service manuals are pricey and many service procedures refer to expensive special tools only dealers have. Owners forums on the web can have some useful tips but coverage is spotty and the quality of the information is only as reliable as its source. Repair manuals sold in auto parts stores seem like a bargain, but tend to have small, dark photos, general procedures written for a wide range of years and models that may or may not apply to your car, and steps that have you jumping back and forth between chapters just to perform one repair operation. And what about the economics of new versus used parts? What advances in aftermarket parts are worth looking into for your car?

Taking input like that into account, Tom Currao and I coauthored HPBooks' *Camaro Restoration Handbook*. First published in 1990, this title focuses on the disassembly and assembly of first-generation (1967–69)

and second-generation (1970–81) Camaros. It addresses the task of a complete road-to-roof restoration, and it is still in print.

HPBooks' *Classic Camaro* is an update of the previously published *Camaro Owner's Handbook*. It too covers 1967–81 Camaros, but with this new title, I've taken a much more visual approach to restoration and weekend projects that you, the owner, are likely to do. It presumes that large, sharp pictures and detailed captions covering every key step are preferable to columns and columns of gray text. There are over 600 photos. Each repair or project starts with a list of the tools and supplies you'll need, so you don't have to run out at 6 p.m. on a Sunday night to try to find that window winder removal tool you didn't know you needed. I have attempted to distill repair tips from experts on what parts wear out, suggest maintenance that can prevent untimely repairs, and give cost-saving advice wherever possible.

Having performed the restoration projects and repairs myself in the process of researching, writing, and illustrating this book, I know you'll find *Classic Camaro* a useful tool and a trusted source. Nearly 45 years ago, General Motors began mass-producing the Camaro as an answer to Ford's Mustang, and except for an eight-year hiatus from 2003 to 2009, the sporty muscle coupe has since been a key attraction in the Chevy showroom. With a little care and maybe some help from this book, you can keep your classic Camaro standing proud and running strong for years to come. So put down the laptop and give your Camaro the attention it deserves. And don't forget your copy of *Classic Camaro*.

—*Ron Sessions*

FINDING A
PROJECT CAR

Chapter 1
How to Buy a Used Classic Camaro

This back-alley 1969 Sport Coupe says "take me home." Sure it's got that neat cowl-induction hood, but look closer and that little cash register in your head should be going...ka-ching, ka-ching! There is a lot of trim missing and every panel has been tweaked this way or that. This, friends, is a parts car. If you want a project car, fine, but don't buy the first one you come across.

Did you really see it or was it just an apparition? There, parked between a rusting AMC Pacer and a guy selling lawn sculptures out of a Jolly Green Giant-colored Corvair Greenbier van, you caught a glimpse of a '69 Camaro with a FOR SALE sign in the windshield. Or did you? There was no stopping now as traffic swept you along, but after work, you'd come back for a better look. Could it be a Rally Sport or Super Sport? The wheels started turning in your head. What color is it? I wonder if it's a big-block car, or maybe a Z28? Is it original? How much do they want for it?

Buying a used Camaro can be a very exciting proposition, what with visions of cruise night runs, car club meets and weekend getaways dancing in your head. But before you reach for your wallet, take a deep breath and ask yourself a few questions.

Do you want to purchase a Camaro to be an everyday driver, own a show-quality car with investment potential or something in between? The answer to this question will skew everything you do to your Camaro while you own it. For that matter, it should be an important factor in the type of Camaro you buy and how much you pay for it. Simply put, a ratty, raced, rusted and clapped-out shell of a Z28, pace car or SS396 might be more desirable to a collector than a clean, unmodified six-cylinder Powerglide Sport Coupe. On the other hand, someone desiring a solid, reliable Camaro to drive might opt for the latter and be dollars ahead.

If you're searching out a basic Camaro to commute and maybe cruise in, your prerequisites for purchasing it are the same as for any other used car. You want a Camaro in solid structural condition. Because the Camaro has a unitized body with a partial front subframe, serious rust or collision damage in the middle or rear underbody can substantially compromise the car's integrity. Unless you're real handy with a welding torch and have access to professional measuring equipment, stay away from a "bent" or "Swiss cheese" Camaro. For a "driver," you want a Camaro that can be maintained with minimum fuss and investment. That means an engine with good compression, no smoke, and all of the emission-control equipment hooked up and functional, fade-free, responsive brakes, no clunks in the drivetrain, no electrical system issues and no wobbles in the suspension or steering. If this particular Camaro has custom "mag" wheels, some chromed parts in the engine bay and a chain-store sound system, who cares? Originality isn't as important as good condition.

Unless you want to perform a restoration, stay away from high-mileage Camaros. Although items such as the front carpeting, driver's seat upholstery, brake and clutch pedals and weatherstripping can be replaced, sellers seldom go to the trouble and expense, and the condition of these is probably a more reliable indicator than what the odometer shows. If the Camaro you're looking at has torn and shabby upholstery, worn-through pedals and driver-footwell carpeting, dried-up door weatherstripping and the odometer reads 55,000 miles, make a mental note. It's probably more like 155,000 miles. Then again, on a 30-year-old car that's

A Camaro that's received obvious care and attention from a private owner such as this Butternut Yellow 1967 Rally Sport is a great way to start a long and lasting relationship. And the seller still has the original window sticker and Protecto-Plate!

Down at the local Garden of Gears, you take your chances with cars prettied up from the auction block.

been kept in service, that kind of mileage is quite possible. Just do the math.

It's been said that "cleanliness is next to godliness," and this time-honored saw applies to Camaros as well. Maybe you're checking out a car that shows a fair amount of carpet wear but the interior isn't littered with Pepsi stains and Taco Bell wrappers. Perhaps the driver's seat has a little tear in the upholstery, but the owner stitched it to keep it from spreading. It's likely there's an assortment of stone chips and parking-lot dings, but someone went to the trouble of touching up the paint and applying a coat of wax. Under the hood, you might find a normal accumulation of oil mist and road grime, but the battery is corrosion-free, the air-cleaner element is fresh and the oil on the dipstick is nearly clear. In the trunk, there's a car cover, the spare holds air and the bumper jack is present and accounted for, too. If the foregoing describes the Camaro you're looking at, buy it. Because if you don't, someone else surely will.

Having just championed the clean car, it is possible for a Camaro to be too clean. Cast a wary eye toward an over-detailed car. Beware of fresh paint or undercoating that may be hiding some big surprises. If the interior of the Camaro you're looking at has so much silicone spray on the dash and door panels that you're barely able to keep the steering wheel from slipping out of your hands, take pause. Or if the engine compartment's been hastily painted with gobs of overspray on wires, belts, hoses and various accessories, take a walk. Usually, you'll find this type of Camaro on a used-car lot from the other side of the tracks.

Some Camaros also make great investments because they are increasing in value as time passes, yet they're reliable enough to be driven on special

occasions without having to be overly fussy about maintenance and storage. Into this category, you can put virtually all 1967–69 Camaros, although obviously Rally Sports, Super Sports, Z28s, pace-car replicas, COPO big-block cars, Yenkos and ZL-1s will appreciate much faster than, say, a nice, clean 6-cylinder convertible. Among the second-generation cars, 1970–74 and 1977 Z28s, 1970–72 SS396s and 1970–73 Rally Sports are much sought after.

The value of any Camaro is really based on the rule of supply and demand. As a rule, limited-production performance models are in greatest demand. Sometimes, it's an unusual color combination that increases a collector's interest. More pedestrian Camaros, such as Sport Coupes with 2-barrel V-8s, may be worth a bundle because they're equipped with lots of options, such as power windows, low-tone exhaust, a fold-down rear seat, tri-volume horn, tilt steering wheel, fiber-optics

The flip-up front end may look cool, but modified cars like this 1970 Camaro, no matter how nicely done, can be tough to register in many states and cost a bundle to put back to stock condition.

The 1969 Camaro Pace Car Replicas are highly sought after, but beware of fakes.

When looking for pedigree, check what the trim tag says against published sources. Trim tags can be counterfeited, however, so if you're looking to spend big for a rare model, verify against the build sheet or broadcast sheet, Protecto-plate and window sticker, if available.

light monitor, 8-track cassette player, disc brakes or inflatable spare tire. The less popular the option originally was, the rarer it is today, which, you guessed it, makes it more valuable.

Big-block Camaros can light the rear tires at will; limited production ensures a fast appreciation curve.

Sight down the side of the car and look for wavy sheet metal.

No matter what any published value guide says, a Camaro is really only worth what a buyer will pay for it. A burned-out hulk of a 1969 Yenko Camaro is probably worth investing in, provided you have the time and money to restore it. A finished, running car with all of its pieces present and accounted for is a lot easier to sell than a pile of parts and promises. But if you are paying a premium for a project car with a pedigree, better check out its papers before shelling out that long green.

Do your homework before venturing out. Consult published sources such as the *Illustrated Camaro Buyer's Guide*, the *Camaro White Book*, the *Camaro Restoration Handbook* and others, as well as *Hemming's Motor News*, *Autoweek* and your local illustrated *Auto Trader* to get a handle on prices. Read all you can about serial numbers and trim tags.

Remember, modified cars are worth less than original ones, no matter how well done. Any time a car is missing any of its original parts or has holes cut in its flanks to install aftermarket equipment, it will cost you money to find and buy the original parts and fix any of the sheet-metal butchery.

Whether you're in the market for a driver or collector car with investment potential, begin your inspection with a quick tour of the Camaro's exterior. Get on your knees and sight down each side of the car. Wavy-looking doors and quarter panels raise the chances this Camaro suffered some collision damage. Crazed, cracking or crowfooted paint is another indicator of a quickie rustout or collision repair. Rap the lower edges of the fenders, doors and rear quarter panels with your knuckles. Healthy sheet metal will emit a hollow sound, while rusty metal will crunch, and plastic filler will sound flat and non-metallic. An old trick is to take along a refrigerator magnet that won't scratch the paint and stick it to those same areas you just rapped. The magnet will fall off areas filled with plastic filler and stick to the good metal.

Be real suspicious of fresh paint. Look for dead giveaways of a cheapie paint job, such as overspray on the fuel tank, weatherstripping, engine compartment, springs, exhaust and door stickers. If the painter couldn't take the time to mask the job properly, imagine what care he used when applying the paint. But more importantly, be suspicious of what the fresh paint may be hiding underneath.

Take note of how the car sits. A Camaro that's leaning to one side may indicate sagging springs or severe structural problems. Push down on each corner of the car and release. If it bobs up and down more than once, new shock absorbers are in the offing. A front end that groans could mean

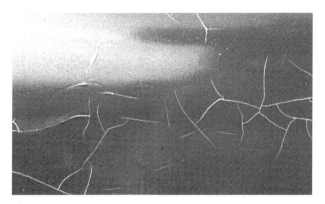

Crowfooted paint indicates a hasty, unprofessional paint job and may signal other hidden sheet-metal abuse.

An old trick when inspecting a car's bodywork is to take a small refrigerator magnet, which sticks to good metal but not to plastic filler. Or better yet, try one of these Spot Rot gauges available from your local auto parts store.

In humid climates and areas where tree droppings accumulate around the windshield and backlite moldings, rust perforation can mean big, expensive repairs.

If the Camaro has a vinyl roof, check for bubbles or tears that indicate that rust has gained a foothold.

worn-out control-arm bushings

Many early Camaros were equipped with vinyl roofs. These are notorious for promoting and hiding rusty steel roofs underneath. If the car you're inspecting has a vinyl roof, check for cracked fabric that would let moisture in. Look carefully for bubbles under the vinyl, especially around the rear window. Push on the roof (and any bubbles you might find) with your fingers. If you hear a crunch, the roof is rusted under the vinyl, requiring expensive repair, perhaps replacement of the entire steel roof. This can take thousands of dollars to fix properly. Walk away from a Camaro with a rusty roof unless it's a rare model or the seller comes way down on price.

About 10 percent of 1967–69 Camaros were convertibles. No convertible models were offered on the 1970–71 second-generation Camaros. A convertible is a wonderful thing on a warm, sunny day or dreamy, starry night. But cutting the roof off any unit-body car—Camaros included—makes for a willowy structure with lots of creaks and groans.

When shopping for a used Camaro convertible, make doubly sure the car has no major rust or collision damage. Check that the top raises, lowers and latches properly and visibility through the plastic rear window isn't unduly impaired. Most Camaros have power-operated tops consisting of electric servos acting on a hydraulic pump and rams. If the seals on any of the hydraulics go south, they can leak smelly, brownish red hydraulic fluid into the rear compartment—a real mess.

From 1978 on, Camaros could be ordered with twin removable glass roof panels. Known as T-tops, these panels gave a convertible-like open-air feeling for the driver and front-seat passenger. Like a pop-up sunroof, the T-top panels indexed on two pins and secured to the windshield header and rear roof section with over-center latches. In time the panels worked loose and rattled and creaked in their mounts. Also, the weatherstripping shrank and caused water leaks and wind noise. Leaking water then warped and delaminated the hardboard headliner, in addition to dripping on the driver's head. When buying a used Camaro with T-tops, check that the glass panels and latches are not damaged. More than likely, the weatherstripping will need to be replaced, along with the discolored and warped headliner which must be custom-fitted.

Aftermarket hood pins look cool but ruin an otherwise perfect hood if you're going for that stock look.

This 1968 convertible could be a dream ride, but a costly one if the top fabric is torn, weatherstripping is cracked or missing, rear window is clouded or yellowed, boot is missing, latches bent or electrical or hydraulic systems not functioning properly.

No matter how nicely done, stay away from cars with aftermarket sunroof conversions. This is just one big, expensive hole in the roof.

Buying a partially disassembled car can be tricky. On one hand, you can see beyond the trim to determine if what's underneath is sound. On the other hand, will you be able to get all of the missing pieces to complete the job?

Scan the bodywork for exterior mods that will be expensive to remedy. A big turnoff is radiused rear fenders or fender flares; putting the quarter panels back to stock is a major undertaking. If the Camaro is equipped with an aftermarket hood scoop or drilled for hood pins, plan on replacing the hood; engine heat and metal flexing from openings and closings mean bodywork to the hood doesn't last. Ditto for a Camaro with an aftermarket sunroof; once that big hole is cut in the roof, the only remedy is welding on a replacement roof and that's major surgery.

Perhaps you're checking out a 1967–69 Rally Sport. If so, make sure the hideaway headlamps are functioning properly by turning the headlamps on and off several times while someone observes up front. Buying all these pieces from scratch (particularly 1968–69 models with vacuum controls) will set you back hundreds, perhaps more than a thousand dollars. And getting these headlamps to work in a non-functioning car is very labor-intensive.

Don't get your knickers in a bind over damaged or missing emblems, chrome trim, lights, bumpers or grille—these can be obtained from GM or Camaro aftermarket parts and accessories outlets. Just deduct their value from the cost of the car.

Have a look inside. If the doors sag as they come off their strikers, new hinge pins and bushings need to be installed. Since the driver's door gets opened and closed many more times than the passenger's

door, that side wears out first. It's a rare Camaro that won't show wear on the soft interior trim parts such as the carpeting, seats, dashpad, package tray, headliner, sun visors and door trim panels (unless it's recently been redone). Even if all the soft trim items are worn, faded or badly cracked, these are easily replaced. Do check, though, for musty, mildewed carpeting that may signal a leaking windshield or rear window, or worst of all, a rusty floor.

Some interior trim pieces, especially faded and cracked ABS plastic parts on early second-generation cars, are difficult to obtain if replacements are needed. If you buy a Sunbelt car, you might consider finding a similar model donor car from the Rustbelt to pick trim pieces off of.

Is the steering wheel cracked? If the wheel rim is shod with an aftermarket laced cover, ask the owner for a look underneath. Most 1967–72 Camaros have cracked steering wheels and these are not

An interior that's intact and shows obvious care should be your clue to the condition of the rest of the car. This 1969 SS350 is clean and shows no unusual wear on carpet or pedals.

On the other hand, this 1973 Type LT cabin looks like it was run hard and put away wet; a jumble of torn fabric, dirty rags, sun-bleached plastic and a collapsed headliner. Plus rear quarter trim panels have been hacked up to install aftermarket speakers.

Traction bars may be the hot ticket down the quarter mile, but their presence suggests previous driveline abuse.

Take a peek inside the trunk. Quite often the trunk floor is rusted through on 1967-69 Camaros, which compromises fuel tank retention and rear suspension integrity.

inexpensive to repair or replace.

Watch out for ham-fisted modifications that will lead to costly repairs. Take a gander at the transmission tunnel and check if it's been cut open for an aftermarket shifter or transmission. Inspect for a dash cut out for an aftermarket radio, gauges or A/C system. Be on the lookout for doors, kick panels, rear shelf or rear quarter-trim panels sliced and diced for speakers.

Take a flashlight and have a look under the dash. If it's a jumble of spliced wires, connectors and electrical tape, you could be buying into a dash wiring-harness job, not to mention a possible fire due to a short-circuit some day! Start the engine and check the gauges, lights, wipers, heater blower and radio for proper operation. If they don't operate, investigate why, and deduct more points.

Open the trunk and have a look. Are all the pieces to the jack there and does the spare have

decent tread or even hold air? Lift up the trunk mat and check the trunk floor for rust—a big problem on 1967–69 cars. A serious rustout here could involve lots of cutting and welding to maintain the integrity of the fuel-tank mounting straps and leaf-spring shackles--big, nasty, expensive repairs. How about the rear wiring harness? Was it cut up to install a trailer harness?

Check the inside of the rear quarter panels and rear end panel for signs of a collision repair. One surefire giveaway is small drill holes with hardened plastic filler oozing through; these tell you the repair was done the slide-hammer and Bondo way, not what you want as a foundation for a restoration.

Time to inspect how things look under the hood. If the engine's caked with oil and dirt, that's an indication of lack of maintenance. Pull the dipstick. White goo at the bottom could be coolant in the crankcase, pointing to a blown head gasket or cracked cylinder head or block. On the other hand, black, gritty oil on the dipstick indicates that it's been a long time since the last oil change, unless the

Slightly less than one-fourth of all first-generation Camaros were 6-cylinder powered. While the Chevy inline-6 is smooth running and durable as an anvil, its collector value is next to nil.

Dusty but all there, this 1967 RS with a 210-hp 2-bbl 327 V-8 has all of the original emission-control hardware intact—stuff that's hard to find in the boneyard.

Pop the radiator cap and take a gander. Rust, white goo or bubbles in the coolant are all signs of trouble.

When possible, put the Camaro on a hoist to check its underpinnings. Look for rustouts, crash damage, leaking vitals, exhaust system integrity.

owner was using graphite motor oil.

If the engine's cool, take a towel and unscrew the radiator cap. If you spot rust here, there's more of it inside the engine, which can eventually clog water jackets and cause overheating. Also, be on the lookout for cracked and leaky radiator and heater hoses.

Is the engine original? Does its VIN match that on the dash or door jamb? If not, is it at least the correct type of engine for this year and model of Camaro? Collectors routinely deduct big points if the two do not match up. Is all of the original emission-control-system hardware in place? If not, this can be a deal-killer in states where it's illegal to register a non-smog-certified car. How about the air cleaner and intake and exhaust manifolds? If you're planning this Camaro for shows, these pieces must be correct and can be a bear to find in salvage yards. Aftermarket speed equipment such as headers, intake systems, and electronic ignition systems may

be OK for a daily driver, but keep in mind the car still must pass any applicable state emission-control inspection or tailpipe checks.

Ask the seller if you can put the Camaro on a lift. If he's honest and has nothing to hide, he shouldn't object. Viewed from underneath, any serious rustouts or crash damage should be readily apparent. Be wary of fresh undercoating on the floorpan. Ask yourself, what could it be hiding? If you spot traction bars, helper springs, air shocks or a trailer hitch, the Camaro's seen tough duty as a quarter-mile pavement burner or a workhorse.

Have a gander at the car's front end. Do the tires show uneven tread wear or cupping? Are the shocks leaking? Is there any rubber left in the sway-bar link bushings? While observing the steering linkage, grab a front tire and move it left and right, in and out. Look for relative movement at the ball joints, tie rods, Pitman arm and idler arm. Are the grease fittings caked over with a buildup of old grease and

Tires this heat-cracked and bald may be indicators of less than current maintenance elsewhere. By all means, check the condition of the brakes, too.

A trailer hitch is a sure sign this 1978 Camaro saw workhorse duty that can strain drivetrain components.

Check the car's serial number or VIN against what's on the title.

dirt? If so, it's been a long time since the last lube job. Are the rubber boots cracked? If grease can get out, water and dirt can get into the joints, accelerating wear. Are the power-steering hoses leaking? A front-end job will set you back many hundreds of dollars.

Moving rearward now, check for engine, transmission and rear-axle leaks. These can be fixed, but it's your driveway or garage floor that's taking a beating in the meantime. And leaks here are indicative of the car's overall condition. So is an exhaust system hung with coat hangers and patched with tape. Also check the fuel and brake lines. The flexible fuel hoses near the gas tank and carburetor eventually will crack and leak, creating a fire danger. Look for drips, but even better, use your nose. If you smell raw gas, there's a leak nearby.

Road Test

Fire up the engine and listen carefully. If you hear the rattle of worn connecting-rod or main bearings in the moments before the engine reaches full oil

pressure, beware of big problems just around the corner. A high-mileage Camaro may emit a characteristic piston slap due to excess clearance or clattering valve lifters due to varnish deposits when the engine's cold—not a deal killer—but items that should be attended to in the next overhaul.

Time to read smoke signals. White smoke in the exhaust of a warm engine could be a blown head gasket or leaking automatic transmission vacuum modulator. A compression test of the engine and a vacuum test of the modulator will settle that question. Black smoke is an over-rich air/fuel mixture and could be a sticking choke or misadjusted carburetor. Blue smoke, however, is burned oil; if the smoke disappears soon after startup, the cause is likely worn valve seals. Blue smoke on a warm engine while downshifting or decelerating indicates worn valve guides.

Always check the brakes for a firm pedal before venturing out. Find a large, empty parking lot for your initial test drive so you can evaluate the Camaro without the distraction of traffic. Also, turn off the radio and keep your ears tuned into the sound the car is making.

It's a good idea to have a friend follow in back to see if the car tracks straight. Does it pull to one side with your hands on or off the wheel? Is there any lag in the steering? Stop and turn the steering wheel to full-right lock, then spin it to full-left lock. Does the power steering chatter and groan? When you hit a pothole or speed bump, or when going up a driveway ramp, do you hear any nasty clunks or groans from the suspension?

Next, see how the Camaro decelerates from moderate speed. Does it stop straight and without juddering? How does the brake pedal feel? If the Camaro's an automatic, are the upshifts and downshifts positive, without slippage? On a stick-shift car, are the synchros in good shape? Does the trans pop out of gear when you decelerate or coast down a hill in gear? Is the clutch slipping or grabbing only at the end of its travel? Or, does the clutch judder even when released smoothly?

Find a quiet, straight stretch of road and listen to the drivetrain. Clicking and rumbling sounds on acceleration may be caused by worn U-joints. Concentrate on the rear axle. Listen for objectionable gear whine. Check if the pitch changes appreciably between acceleration, steady-state and coasting cycles.

If this Camaro still looks good after all of your poking and probing, then start thinking about making the seller an offer. At the very least, you now have a better idea of what your Camaro project will entail.

Open every nook and cranny and poke around. If the owner has nothing to hide, he won't mind. Once you're sure this is the Camaro you want to plunk the long green down on, and it passed all of the checks I've recommended, then it deserves a new home—yours.

INTERIOR

Chapter 2
How to Install a Dashpad

1. Sun-bleached and cracked vinyl dashpad on this '67 Rally Sport spoils an otherwise attractive interior.

One of the first safety features was the padded dashboard. Along with seatbelts, this item became a standard feature on most cars in the late 1950s. The pad gets little or no wear because barring a serious accident, nothing comes in contact with it. But sitting as it does atop the instrument panel and under the windshield, it gets bombarded with solar radiation day after day.

On 1967–69 and 1979–81 Camaros the dashpad is foam-backed vinyl. In time, exposure to the sun bakes the plasticizers out of the vinyl causing it to split. Then the foam underneath dries out and leaks like sand. The urethane dashpad on 1970–78 models is more durable, but eventually its edges warp and the rubberized material blackens.

Replacing the dashpad on any 1970–81 Camaro is a large undertaking because the padded material forms the major part of the structure and carries the gauges and controls. So the entire instrument panel, gauges, heater/air-conditioning controls, radio and control switches for lights, wipers and so on must be disassembled. For a detailed description of this procedure, see my *Camaro Restoration Handbook*, also published by HPBooks.

First-generation Camaros have it much easier. Because the steel part of the dash carries most of the components on 1967–69 models, just the padded section up top needs to be replaced. On these Camaros, the dashpad is retained to the steel dashboard with stud nuts. Getting at these stud nuts usually requires removing the glove box door and liner, heater/air-conditioning controls and possibly some ductwork, as well as dropping down the steering column and

pulling the instrument binnacle out a few inches from the dash. On top, the A-pillar trim moldings will also have to be removed. Follow along as we replace the cracked dashpad on a 1967 Rally Sport with a reproduction unit from Classic Industries.

Tools & Supplies Needed
- Phillips-head screwdriver
- Small deep-well socket set (3/8" or 1/4" drive)
- Assortment of small open-end and box-end wrenches

2. To gain access to the dashpad stud nuts, start by removing two screws retaining trim moldings to A-pillars and lift off.

3. Remove the glove box hinge screws and lift off the glove box door.

4. Remove the Phillips-head screws retaining the glove box liner and remove the liner. Also, on 1967–68 cars so equipped, remove the two A/C outlet ball vents (two screws) and disconnect the ducts.

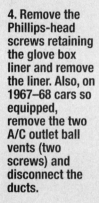

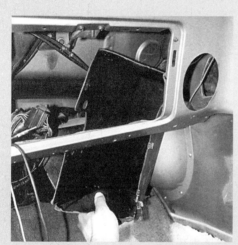

5. Pull off the two radio shaft knobs and remove the large diameter shaft nuts.

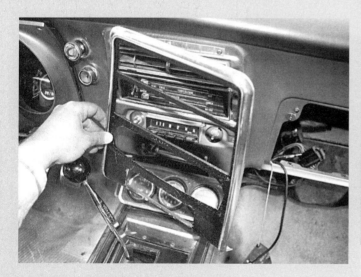

6. Remove the Phillips-head screws at the bottom of the center trim panel and lift off the panel.

7. On A/C cars, there's a lot of ducting in the way. It has to come out of 1967–68 cars to get at the dashpad's stud nuts.

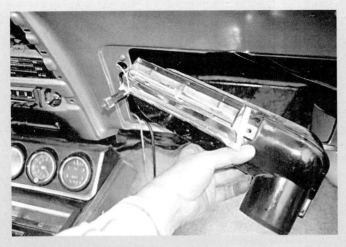

8. Next, remove the small hex screws for the center A/C outlet (if so equipped) and slide out the outlet.

9. Remove the nuts under the dash supporting the steering column and let the column sag a few inches. This will provide clearance to slide the gauges away from the dash far enough to get a wrench on the dashpad stud nuts.

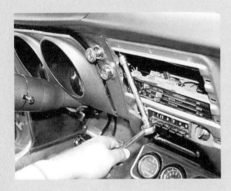

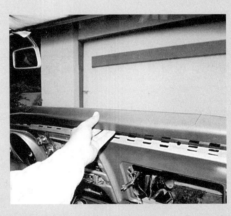

10. With a small socket (1/4" or 5/16") and long extension, remove the dashpad stud nuts. On an original GM dashpad, there may be as many as seven stud nuts to remove.

11. Lift off the old dashpad.

12. Clean the metal dash with Windex or equivalent and a clean cotton cloth.

13. New reproduction dashpad from Classic Industries has just four stud nuts to install.

14. New dashpad fits perfectly. Start each stud nut by hand, then snug down with a wrench or socket, but don't overtighten.

15. Finish buttoning up the dash and you've got a fresh new perspective on the world out there in front of your Camaro's dashboard.

Chapter 3

Steering Wheel Repair

1. To fix a cracked steering wheel, you must remove it from the car. Disconnect the battery. Start by popping off the horn button with a flat-blade screwdriver.

It's doubtful that you'll interact with any other part of your Camaro more than its steering wheel. Going "behind the wheel" or "taking the wheel" is a time-worn euphemism for driving. Time, temperature extremes and exposure to sunlight also do their part to wear away at the steering wheel. This is particularly true of 1967–72 Camaros with a hard-plastic, steel-cored steering wheel which tends to develop multiple cracks and fractures in the plastic (1973-and-later models have a molded urethane wheel that holds up better over time).

Cruising the boneyards for a crack-free example is a fruitless exercise because any wheel you might find will suffer the same malady—unless of course you were to find a low-mileage Camaro someone tucked away in a vault and convince the owner to sell you just the steering wheel. Dream on. Your only other options are buying a new wheel or fixing yours. New steering wheels are available from Camaro mail-order parts outlets, but reproductions of original-style wheels are available for only a few years and models. Most attractive among these are the simulated wood-rimmed wheels with brushed aluminum center spokes that were optional on 1967–69 Camaros. But if your Camaro didn't come from the factory with a wood wheel and you're a stickler about originality, you'll need to fix your existing wheel.

Cracks in hard-plastic steering wheels can be repaired with epoxy. The procedure involves grinding a V-shaped notch into the plastic as deep as the fracture goes, filling with epoxy, sanding, filing, priming and painting. You'll repeat this latter part as many times as it takes to get a smooth, good-looking wheel.

Tools & Supplies Needed
- Steering wheel puller
- Flat blade screwdriver
- Phillips-head screwdriver
- Ratchet and socket set
- Coarse flat file
- Small rat tail file
- Dremel tool
- Hacksaw
- Small rotary sander
- Sandpaper (80- to 400-grit)
- PC7 Epoxy
- Putty knife or kitchen knife
- Silicone/grease remover/surface prep
- Lacquer thinner
- Polyester flexible primer/plastic prep
- SEM vinyl and plastic color spray

This must be done with the wheel off the car, so you'll need to remove it with a puller. Before pulling the wheel, be sure to disconnect the battery and remove the horn ring or button and horn contact components.

The process of finding and grinding out the cracks can be very time-consuming, as will the sanding and filing once the epoxy has had a chance to harden. Don't try to do the entire operation in one day.

2. With a Phillips-head screwdriver, remove the screws for the horn actuating mechanism. Take note of how it all fits together so the horn will work again later.

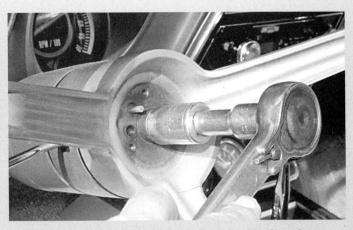

3. Remove the nut retaining the steering wheel to the column.

4. The steering wheel is a taper fit on the column splines, so it won't just lift off. Sometimes you can bump it off with your knees while lifting the wheel with steady pressure. The easiest removal method is to use a steering wheel puller. Carefully thread two bolts from the puller at least three turns into the wheel hub, then tighten the center screw until the wheel pops free.

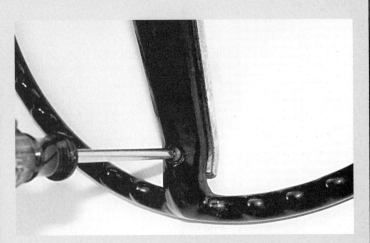

5. Horn ring and spoke trim attaches with Phillips-head screws from the rear. Remove these.

6. Crack city. Here's a big one where a spoke meets the hub.

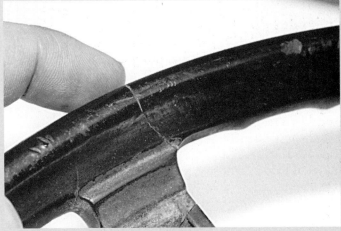

7. Don't overlook these hairline cracks on the rim. Sometimes these are hidden by a buildup of dirt and body oil from your hands.

8. To repair a crack, you must temporarily make it worse by opening it up into a V-shape groove so epoxy can be applied. You can use a hacksaw or a Dremel tool for really precision work. Cut as deep as you must to get to the bottom of the crack.

9. The Eastwood Company sells a steering-wheel repair kit that includes enough PC7 2-part epoxy to fix several wheels. You'll need a clean piece of cardboard and a putty or kitchen knife to mix equal parts of plastic and catalyst.

10. Clean the wheel with an oil and silicone remover like Eastwood's PRE before applying epoxy.

11. Apply the epoxy to the V-grooved areas of the wheel using a small screwdriver.

12. With a finger dipped in lacquer thinner, shape the epoxy while it's still wet and pliable. This will reduce the amount of filing and sanding required later on.

13. Allow the epoxy to cure for at least two days before sanding and filing. On flat surfaces in open areas of the wheel, a coarse flat file makes progress quickly.

14. For detail work and around corners, use a small, tapered-nose flat file and a rat tail (round) file.

15. Follow this with sandpaper, first coarse, then medium and finally fine.

16. After final sanding with 400-grit wet/dry paper, clean the wheel with a degreaser/dewaxer such as Eastwood's PRE, then prime the wheel with a solvent-based self-etching primer.

17. Finally, apply a color coat of flexible SEM vinyl and plastic color spray followed by two coats of clear.

18. When done, your vintage Camaro steering wheel will look as good as new.

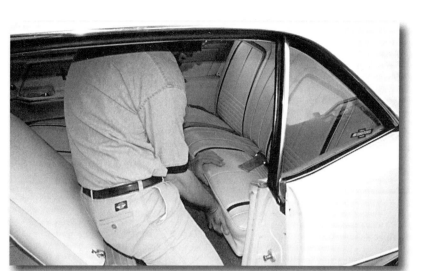

1. Your Camaro's rear package shelf is easy to get to once the rear seat is removed. The rear cushion comes out first. It's held in place by sheet-metal hooks in the floor that grab the seat's metal frame. To remove the rear cushion, push it straight back firmly with one hand while lifting it up with your other hand. It'll take a few attempts until you get the hang of it.

Chapter 4

Installing a Rear Package Tray

Like the dashpad, your Camaro's rear package shelf behind the rear seat gets baked by the sun and sometimes gets exposed to water, discoloring and warping in the process. Often, the panel has been cut up by a previous owner to install aftermarket audio speakers. It consists of a vinyl- or fabric-covered sheet of cardboard with a loose strip of foam-backed vinyl sewn onto its leading edge where it meets the rear seatback.

Replacing the rear package shelf is one of the easier weekend projects you can do on your Camaro. Merely remove the rear seat to gain access, then slide a putty knife between the shelf and the rear bulkhead sheet metal to break the adhesive bond holding it in position. If aftermarket speakers are mounted on the package shelf, the grilles for these will have to be removed first. Ditto for second-generation cars with the forced-air-type rear window defogger.

If your car's existing package shelf is just faded, but not warped or torn up, you can remove it and spray it with vinyl dye for a fresh appearance. New package shelves are available in most original 1967–81 Camaro colors from all major Camaro mail-order parts houses. You can go the stock route and get a die-cut original-style package shelf, or for a little more money, you can get a fabric-mesh-covered shelf with speaker cutouts, which eliminates the need to use external speaker grilles. Another option is jute padding. Although not original equipment on your Camaro, the pad helps absorb unwanted road noise from the trunk area and fits under the package shelf. A "sound" investment!

Tools & Supplies Needed
- Socket set (3/8" drive)
- Putty knife
- Phillips-head screwdriver
- Spray adhesive
- Scissors
- Felt-tip pen
- Mat knife or X-Acto

2. Slide the cushion (or cushions in the case of 1970–81 models) out the door and remove the two hex screws retaining the rear seatback to the floor pan.

3. Lift the rear seatback off its three hooks and angle it out through the door opening, taking care not to scrape the rear quarter trim panels.

4. Originally, all Camaros had this cardboard sheet trunk divider, but it's often long gone in cars that led a hard life. Basically, it just tidies up the appearance from inside the trunk, hiding the seat springs. If it's missing, new ones, die-cut to fit, are available. You can also get jute padding for this divider, which will help soundproof the rear of the car.

5. Remove any speakers and their grilles, and rear defogger (some 1970–81 models only).

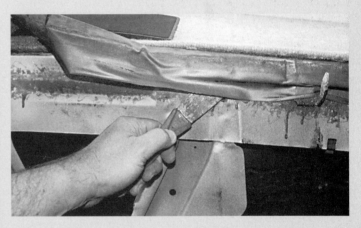

6. Usually, the rear package tray is retained only by adhesive along its leading edge. Run a putty knife between the rear bulkhead and upholstery strip to break the adhesive bond, then lift off what's left of the old material.

7. If you will be cutting holes in the new package tray for speakers or a defogger duct, use the old tray as a template.

8. Because jute padding under the package tray wasn't factory installed, some trays won't fit properly with the jute behind it, especially if the jute is too thick. So do a trial-fit first before applying any adhesive. Also note that rear speakers won't sound their best if they're covered with the padding.

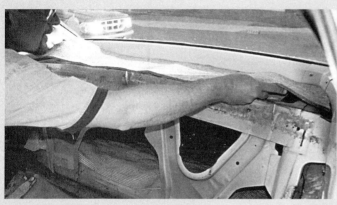

9. If you decide to use the jute backing, give both it and the rear bulkhead a light coating of spray adhesive. After the adhesive "tacks" for a half-minute or so, lay the jute mat down and work out the wrinkles.

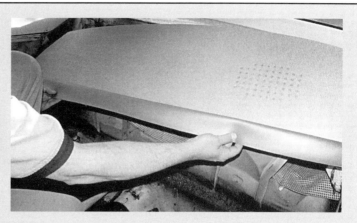

10. Place the new package tray in position and check for fit.

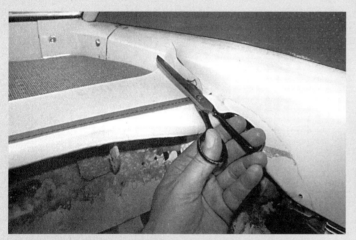

11. Our deluxe-mesh tray with speaker cutouts from Classic Industries fits perfectly after a little trimming in the corners with scissors.

12. We chose not to use the jute pad due to rear speakers being installed, so we sprayed the rear bulkhead and the underside of the new package tray with 3M contact adhesive.

13. Position the new pad firmly against the rear window molding. Then hit the backside of the padded-vinyl trim piece and the top edge of the bulkhead again with adhesive.

14. Finally, fold the trim piece into a nice, uniform scroll-shaped curve just above the three hooks for the rear seatback. Now you're ready to install the back seat and the job is done.

Chapter 5
Installing New Carpet

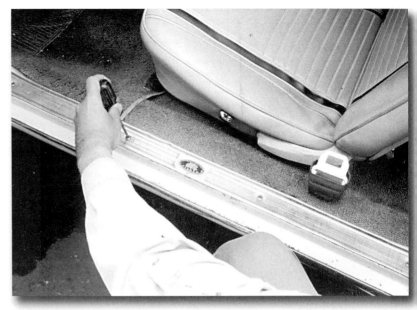

1. The carpeting in this Camaro wasn't threadbare, but sun-faded and stained beyond cleaning. Start by removing the Phillips-head screws and lifting off the sill trim plates.

Over the years, your Camaro's carpeting takes a real beating. You track in leaves, mud, snow and road salt, not to mention coffee and soda-pop spills, and cigarette burns. The fibers get water-soaked, sun-bleached, compacted and ground under the heels of countless shoes. Sooner or later, the carpet becomes threadbare and holes appear, usually in the driver's footwell.

Installing new carpeting is an easy weekend project, requiring no special tools. Today, molded original-equipment-quality carpeting is available in a rainbow of colors from numerous Camaro parts suppliers. The best carpet sets cost about $100 and include heavy jute padded backing, color-keyed driver's heel pad and headlight-dimmer grommet on pre-1976 models. Don't settle for less than factory-original 80-percent nylon/20-percent rayon blend; loop-style on 1967–75 Camaros and cut-pile from 1976.

Getting to the carpeting requires removing the seats, console, shifter boot, seatbelts, sill plates, firewall protector and rear-quarter trim panels, but you probably want to clean, refurbish or replace some of these items anyway. The kick panels can stay in, but should be loosened to sneak some carpet under them.

Camaro carpeting is in two sections; the front overlaps the rear section underneath the seats. Take out the front section first, then the rear. Save the old carpeting for comparison purposes until you've checked the new set for fit. While the carpet's out, inspect the underlayment. This consists of a half-dozen or so pieces of petroleum-based, plastic-backed insulation. If this material is cracked, dried-out, has a rusty color or is missing, you'll need to replace it. If it's in good shape, leave it alone, as the tar-like paper is very messy to work with and has to be scraped out. When installing new underlayment, leave it in the sun or heat it with a hair dryer to make it pliable so it conforms more easily to the floor pan

Tools & Supplies Needed

- Socket set and ratchet
- Open-end wrenches
- Scissors
- Matte knife
- Ice pick or awl
- Chalk
- 3M spray trim adhesive
- Phillips-head screwdriver
- Vacuum cleaner
- Window clip removal tool

contours. Check for floor rust and if all is OK, give the interior a thorough vacuuming.

If you find any rust, fix it now. Remove light surface rust with naval jelly or any of the commercially available rust stabilizers. Actual holes compromise the structural integrity of your car and the only way to fix them is to cut out the rusted sections and weld in new ones. Don't even think of doing a fiberglass patch and Bondo quickie job here. After making the repair, prime and paint the floor and be sure to find the entry point for all that moisture that caused the rust in the first place. This means checking all weatherstripping and on convertibles, the top as well.

When it comes time to install your new carpeting, start with the rear section, then do the front. Required tools include common hand tools and on second-generation Camaros, a Torx-head socket for the seatbelt bolts. For really tough carpet wrinkles, you might want to have some 3M spray trim adhesive on hand.

3. Unbolt the seatbelts. 1967–69 Camaros use hex bolts while seatbelts on 1970–81 models are retained with Torx-head bolts.

2. Moving seats all the way forward aids access to rear bolts. Lift out the front seats.

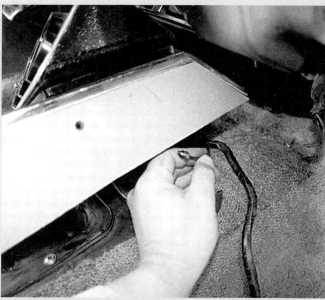

4. Floor shifter and console (if so equipped) are next out. See page 33 in the console repair section for details. If yours is an early model with an oil-pressure gauge in the console, don't forget to disconnect and plug this oil line. A leaky oil line had discolored this Camaro's carpeting.

5. Remove the rear seat cushion by pushing it rearward with your knee to disengage it from its floor hooks, then lift upward.

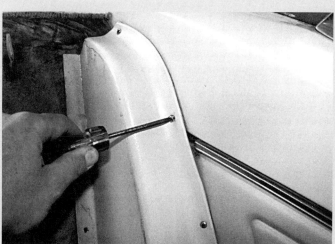

6. Rear quarter trim comes out next. On 1967–69 models, remove the Phillips-head screws at the rear...

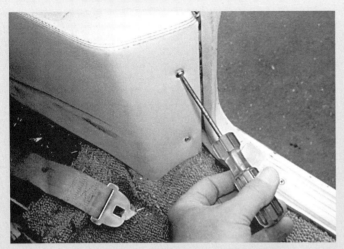

7. ...and the front of each trim panel.

8. Then remove the rear quarter window winders with this special tool.

9. Pull off the door opening windlace. Be gentle with push-on molding as replacements are expensive. Then lift out the rear quarter trim panels.

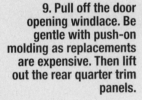

10. Merely loosen front kick panels to sneak carpet out from underneath.

11. Unbolt carpet protector/toe pad, then with seats and console removed, slide out front and rear carpet sections.

12. Vacuum floor and check condition of carpet underlayment.

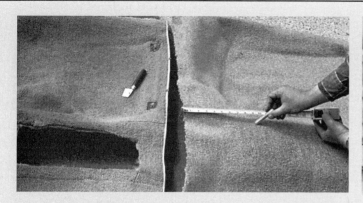

13. Preformed loop-pile carpet from Classic Industries matched up perfectly with the old carpet. Before installing the front section, make cut for console and shifter, if equipped, using the old carpet as a template.

14. Install rear carpet section first, centering it on transmission tunnel. Work wrinkles outboard to door openings. Mark areas to be cut out for console brackets or shifter with chalk. Never trim excess carpet off under sill plates or kick panels until you've installed the seats because the seat bolts draw the carpet inboard.

15. If new carpet set doesn't have this dimmer-switch grommet on pre-'76 Camaros, transfer old one.

16. Temporarily install sill plates to hold outboard ends of carpet in position. Find seat mounting, console and seatbelt bolt holes by poking with an ice pick.

17. Enlarge these holes with a scissors so bolts can be installed without fouling threads with carpet filaments. Install the seatbelts.

18. Tuck carpeting under kick panels with a large putty knife.

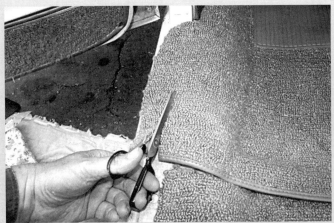

19. Once seat bolts are installed (to draw carpeting down tight), temporarily remove sill plates and do final trim at outboard edges of sills, kick panels, and rear quarter trim panels.

20. New carpeting not only looks great but also gives your vintage Camaro that new-car smell!

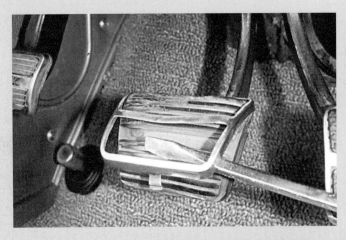

21. With the seats out, it is a good time to dress up the pedals. A deluxe pedal trim kit from Year One is just the ticket. First pry off the old bright trim molding and pull off the old rubber.

22. To ease installation of new rubber, spray some silicone on the pedals. Hook one side, spread it wide then slip the rubber over the opposite lip. It takes a few times to install the first time you try because the rubber's so tight. Then install a new bright trim molding and crimp its tabs over the back of the pedal. Repeat for the remaining pedals.

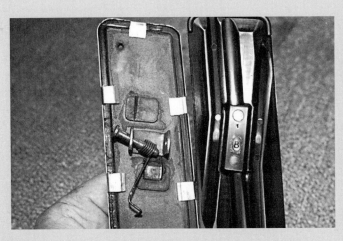

23. Accelerator is toughest to install because it's hard to hook a tension spring on linkage. I did it in-car, but some restorers like to remove the complete throttle linkage and do it on a bench.

24. Fresh pedal pads are the icing on the cake of new carpeting.

Chapter 6

Replacing the Headliner

1. Regardless of headliner type, the first thing you must do is remove the headliner trim moldings. These may be attached with Phillips-head screws, as on mid-1973 to 1981 models...

Although you never walk, sit or come in regular contact with your Camaro's headliner, Old Man Time has a way of taking the newness out of things. Decades of exposure to searing heat, freezing cold, blowing dust, cigarette smoke and reflected sunlight can fade, discolor and dry out that thin layer of cloth, vinyl or fiberboard between your noggin and GM sheet metal. Add in an accidental shunt from an umbrella, 2x4, pool cue, or other long, pointy object, and a headliner's life span looks shorter than white linen at a blueberry pie eating contest. As little tears grow into big rips and strips of fabric hang down, obscuring your view of the road, a decomposing headliner can become hazardous.

Basically, two types of headliners have been used in Camaros: a cut-and-sew fabric type on 1967–73 models that's strung over steel rods, stretched and "hung" in position; and a vinyl-covered fiberboard type on mid-1973-and-later models that's held in place by trim moldings and the dome light.

Removing the fiberboard-type headliner is a no-brainer. Once you've removed the dome light, coat hooks, sun visors, front shoulder-belt anchors and trim moldings that surround the headliner, it drops right out. With the front seats removed, bow the headliner slightly and wrestle it out the door. No special tools are required. But be gentle with it. You can't buy a new fiberboard headliner but you can recover the old one with new material that comes in a kit. Break off a corner and that option disappears. You need good fiberboard as a foundation, so if yours is crumbly, find another used one from a donor car.

To recover the fiberboard, first scrape off the old cloth or vinyl material and as much of the old adhesive as possible. Because it's difficult to work with such a large object and keep it aligned, get a helper. Lay out the old fiberboard and new

material face down and spray them with interior trim contact adhesive. Allow a minute or so for the adhesive to "tack." Working from the center out, lay the new fabric on the fiberboard, taking care to eliminate wrinkles and air bubbles. Once it's straight, fold the material over the edges and glue them in place. If done correctly, the new material fits tightly and seamlessly over the fiberboard and looks like new.

Another way to go on mid-1973 to 1981 Camaros is to install a reproduction headliner kit, such as that offered by Classic Industries (about $60). It includes its own wide, built-in plastic bows, plastic clips, and completely retrofits the mid-1973 to 1981 fiberboard headliner with a factory-look cut-and-sew type.

If you're replacing the cut-and-sew fabric headliner on a 1967–69 or 1970–73 Camaro, the procedure is straightforward. The experts at Year One, Inc. specify Premier Perforated vinyl for 1967–69 standard and 1970–73 custom interior; Impala Leatherette for 1967 custom interior; Bedford Ribbed for 1968–69 custom interior; and Premier Non-perforated for 1970–73 standard interior. If in doubt, snip off a piece from the old headliner and send it in with your order. On 1967–69 models, I highly recommend spending the extra money for the deluxe headliner kit (about $60), which includes new matching sail panels (the upholstered panels inside the rear roof pillars); it's nearly impossible for the novice to recover these oddly shaped pieces successfully without wrinkles.

As for the sun visors, these are sold separately ($60–70 a pair), and should be replaced in most cases along with the headliner for a good color/pattern match. Don't try to whip up a pair of these on your home sewing machine; the factory visors are double stitched and new bushings keep them from tilting down in your face at every bump in the road.

Remember, you'll be working on your back most of the time, arms held above your head until they get stiff. Gravity is working against you; if a corner pops loose, it falls in your face. To put this in context, cut-and-sew headliner installation was the last skilled trade job in Detroit's assembly plants. Nevertheless, if you can hog-ring a seat cover into place or tackle other interior restoration projects, with patience, neatness and a few special tools, you can install a new fabric headliner.

Tools & Supplies Needed
- Headliner kit in proper color and grain
- Trim adhesive, 4-oz. brushable or aerosol can
- Angled trim tucking knife or putty knife
- Curved awl or pick
- Scissors
- Phillips-head screwdriver
- Socket set (1/4" drive)
- Small open-wrench set

2. ...or be a push-on vinyl or plastic windlace, as on this 1969 Camaro...

3. ...or barbed metal fasteners that are released by inserting a flat blade between the headliner and molding and depressing a metal tang, as along the sides of the headliner on 1970–73 models.

4. Don't try to pull loose the A-pillar reveal molding on 1970–73 models until you've removed the Phillips-head screw at the outer lower edge of the molding and hidden under the door weatherstripping.

5. Disconnect the battery, then pry off the dome-light lens, remove its two attaching screws, squeeze the lamp contacts slightly, and free the dome-light base from the wire leads.

6. Remove the sun visors and tape the retaining screws to the bases so they don't get lost. Do the same with the coat hooks and rear-view mirror on 1967–69 cars.

7. Remove Phillips-head screws and lift off cover for shoulder-belt retractor on 1975–81 models. Leave the retractor in place.

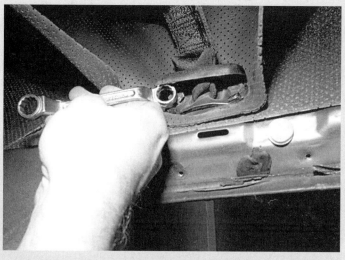

8. On 1974-and-earlier Camaros, however, shoulder-belt anchors must be unbolted. Keep these special high-strength bolts with the shoulder-belt assembly.

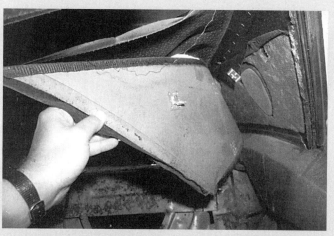

9. Fiberboard sail panels on 1967–69 models damage easily when they're removed. Run a long, flat-blade screwdriver down between the sail panel and C-pillar to release aluminum retaining clips so they don't tear fiberboard backing.

10. Also be gentle when removing sail panels of 1970–81 models. The plastic gets brittle with age and sunlight exposure.

11. Fiberboard headliner on mid-1973 to 1981 models comes out as one piece.

12. To remove a cut-and-sew fabric headliner, first pull edges loose. Use a curved awl if necessary.

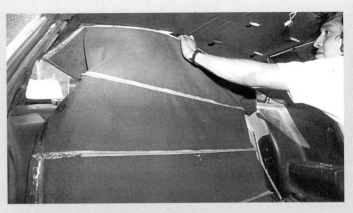

13. With edges free, old headliner hangs from its five listing wires or rods (inside cloth runners). One row at a time, pry wires out of plastic retainer clips in roof (about four to a row) and discard old headliner. Save listing wires for use in replacement headliner.

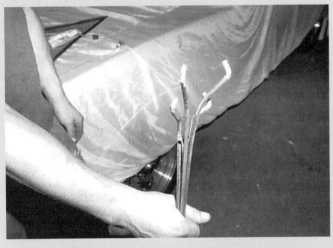

14. Listing wires in 1967–69 Camaros are different lengths. Number them with a felt-tip pen so they can be reused in original holes.

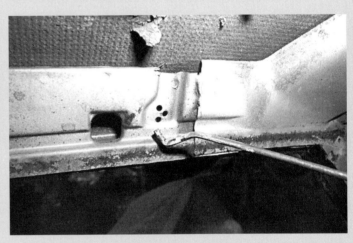

15. On 1967–69 Camaros, front listing wire has multiple holes to allow adjustments for a tighter fit.

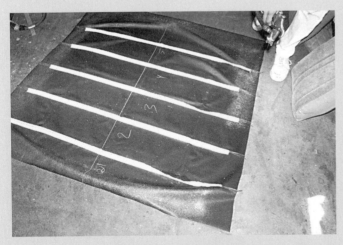

16. Lay out the replacement headliner and apply trim cement to outer 5–6". Also mark headliner centerline with chalk to help align it once inside the car.

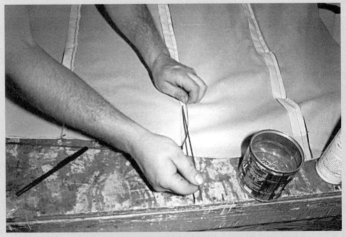

17. Slide listing wires into headliner. These 1970–73 wires are straight and all the same length. On Classic Industries' replacement headliners for mid-1973 to 1981 models, listings are pre-sewn into fabric.

18. Headliner won't hang properly if these plastic retaining clips are broken or missing. You'll need about five rows of four clips.

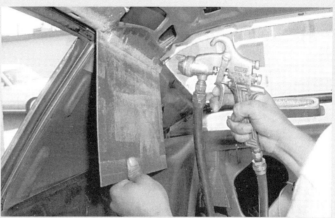

19. Apply trim cement (brush-on type is OK as well) to the 2–3" of sheet metal around the edges of the inner roof panel.

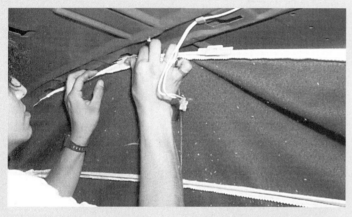

20. Begin installing headliner, rear bow first, by pushing cloth-surrounded listing wires into plastic clips. This is harder than it looks because the headliner wants to fall down, clips slide and fall out of their T-shaped channels and your thumbs get tired of pushing. Use soapy water to coax stubborn listings into clips. Also, cut small slit in headliner for dome light-lead wire where it won't show.

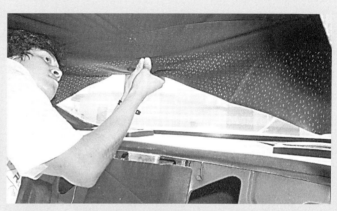

21. Stretch headliner with your thumbs so it's taut and free of wrinkles. You get one shot at this as each section is stretched into position and the trim adhesive on the roof and headliner make contact—first the rear, then the sides and finally the front. If you pull any sections apart for adjustments, you must reapply adhesive.

22. Methodically work the headliner edges into roof channel with a curved putty knife or tucking tool, keeping the fabric taut all the while. On curved sections, cut slits in fabric to make it more pliable.

23. Over the windshield and backlite and inside the C-pillar, tuck the headliner into the steel channels.

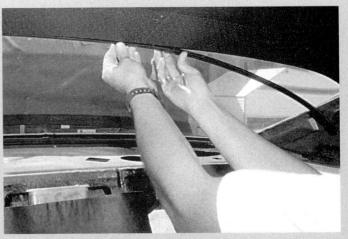

24. Use razor to cut off excess headliner material before installing trim moldings.

25. Where vinyl moldings or windlace is used to retain headliner edges, push it all the way on so lip seats in channel.

26. Use an awl or icepick to find screw holes in the roof for the trim moldings, sun visors, coat hooks and dome light.

27. After installing the dome light, sail panels and other trim pieces, you can sit back and feel satisfied. Things are looking up for your Camaro.

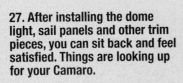

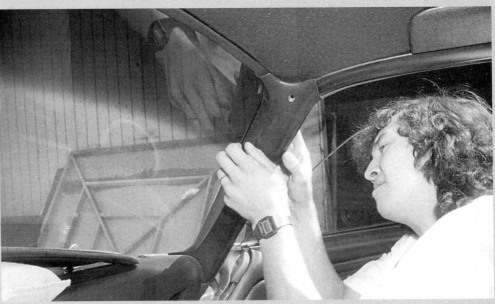

1. The console in Marty Foltz's '68 SS396 was cracked and suffering from previous abuse and it was a perfect candidate for plastic welder repairs. To start, remove the screws for the shifter plate (and boot if it's a manual) and lift out the plate.

Chapter 7

Console Repair & Plastic Welding

In the 1967–81 period, just four different console designs were used on Camaros. For 1967, the console was a two-piece unit with a die-cast metal top and ABS plastic lower section. The 1968–69 Camaro console was similar to the 1967, but both top and bottom halves of the shell were ABS plastic. In the years 1970–72, the console frame was again made of hard ABS plastic, but was a four-piece unit with a single molded top section and screw-on side and rear sections. Beginning in 1973, Camaro switched to the "Firebird" style console, a one-piece molded urethane unit covered in padded, soft vinyl.

Generally, the console houses the manual or automatic gear shifter, a small secondary glove box and an ashtray. Also, consoles could be fitted with optional auxiliary gauges or a clock (1967–69), or power window switches (1973–81). The 1968–69 and 1970–72 consoles have clips to latch the inboard seatbelt buckles when not in use and 1967–69 consoles feature a courtesy lamp for the rear seat area.

Over the years, the console is subjected to intense heat and sunlight, as well as all types of manmade abuse. Plus, the glove box and ashtray lid hinges, latches, rubber stoppers and springs get worn out with normal use.

By far, the most common damage areas are stress cracks in the shell, and broken mounting flanges and stripped screw holes due to overtightened fasteners. So the question is, do you repair it or replace it?

For a 1968–69 Camaro, you can purchase a complete reproduction unit, but it's pricey. Some companies offer a 1968–69 console assembly that's a turnkey deal and includes the injection-molded two-piece ABS shell, floor mounting bracket, metal glove box and ashtray lids, glove box hinge, ashtray receiver, woodgrain trim, emblem, shifter plate (with lens and backing plate on automatics), all necessary springs, screws and rubber stoppers. Or you can just replace the shell

and transfer the other salvageable pieces from your old console and buy new console trim parts on a piecemeal basis. It comes only in black, so if your worn-out console is another color, you'll have to dye it.

If your 1968–69 console is structurally sound but just needs some cosmetic attention, clean it thoroughly with a silicone and wax remover such as Eastwood's PRE, then spray the plastic shell and metal glove box and ashtray lids with black semi-gloss interior lacquer. Finish it off with woodgrain appliqués for the shifter plate and forward trim plate and a new console emblem, and off you go. For models with console-mounted gauges, the gauge plastic lenses (which cloud and get scratched over time), bezel, gauge base, wiring harness, oil line and individual gauges are available separately.

Parts for the one-piece vinyl-covered urethane console used in 1973–81 Camaros (and Firebirds from 1970 on) are readily available, which is fortunate because its shell and glove box lid are virtually impossible to repair satisfactorily. Cracks in the urethane shell understructure can be repaired with SEM-Weld and tears in the vinyl skin bonded together using a vinyl upholstery repair kit, but once the thin layer of foam padding in the middle starts leaking out, the console is basically a write-off. Replacing everything separately on a basket-case 1973–81 console will easily put a major dent in your wallet. Most 1973–81 consoles were black, but in the later years were available in a rainbow of colors. All replacement console shells are black, so spray with interior dye to match existing interior color scheme, if necessary.

Precious few parts are available for 1967 or 1970–72 Camaro consoles. This is largely a moot point on 1967 models because the console's die-cast top section and shifter trim plate and steel glove box and ashtray doors are rarely damaged and can be painted with semi-gloss black for a like-new appearance. On 1970–72 models, the padded glove box lid and plastic shifter plates are available, but beyond that you're stuck with cruising the junkyards and swap meets for good used parts.

The hard ABS plastic shell on 1968–69 models, 1970–72 models, and the lower half of 1967 models can be repaired using Insta-Weld adhesives or by plastic welding. By far, plastic welding is the more durable repair. A good airless plastic welder such as the 80-watt Mini-Weld Model IV sold by the Eastwood Company comes with a selection of rods and tips as well as a detailed instruction booklet. It costs about as much as a new console shell, but can be used over and over again to make other repairs to grilles, dash-panel pieces and lots of other plastic parts.

Basically, plastic welding involves heating filler material and the surrounding plastic until the two melt together and fill in the damaged area. It's first necessary to identify the type of plastic to be repaired (in order to select the correct rod) by color, flexibility, usage or by cutting off a sliver, exposing it to a flame and observing how it burns. ABS plastic used in most Camaro consoles is hard, white in color, used for interior trim parts and burns with thick, black smoke.

Once identified, clean the part to be repaired with soap and water or a silicone-and-oil removing agent such as Eastwood's PRE. With a Dremel tool, create V-grooves in the cracks (on both sides), then fill with ABS rod carefully fed through the welding rod tip. Try practicing on the inside surfaces of the console first until your technique is good enough to try it on the outside where mistakes will be harder to hide. After the plastic has cooled, sand with 80-grit, then 180-grit, until you achieve a smooth contour. Spray on self-

Tools & Supplies Needed	
• Phillips-head screwdriver	• Uni-Weld ribbon
• Socket set	• Dremel tool
• Small nut-driver set	• Electric drill
• Needle-nose pliers	• Sandpaper (80- and 180-grit)
• Mini Weld plastic welder	• PRE surface cleaner
• ABS plastic welding rod	• Self-etching primer
• Steel screen	• Black semi-gloss interior lacquer

etching primer, then two finish coats of semi-gloss black interior lacquer.

If your Camaro's hard-plastic console has attaching flanges broken off or missing chunks, a different repair is called for. Cut some steel mesh (included with welder) to cover both sides of the repair area. Using the broad, flat welding tip, heat the mesh until it melts into the plastic. Then apply Uni-Weld ribbon (a universal plastic welding rod) to the mesh and melt it into the repair area. Finally, redrill any holes for attaching screws. Sand and paint as described above.

Reassemble the console using the new or refurbished parts. And take care not to overtighten the attaching screws that may have cracked the console in the first place! Now follow along as we repair a cracked console in a 1968 Camaro SS396.

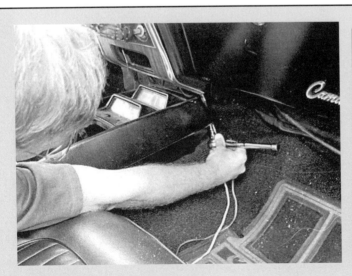

2. Remove all of the fasteners retaining the upper section to the lower one.

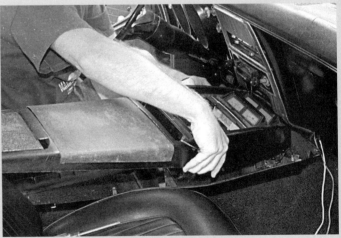

3. Separate the upper console section from the lower.

4. Remove screws for console gauge bezel and lift off bezel.

5. Flip console over and remove screws for console gauge housing. Remove the gauges, but leave them connected to the car.

6. Remove the hex screws retaining the console lower section to the floor.

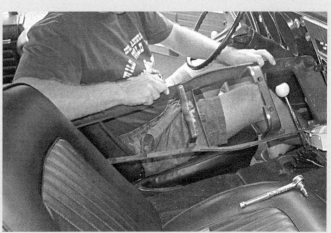

7. Lift out the console lower section.

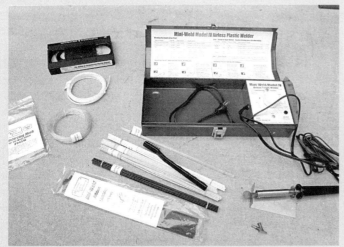

8. Our weapon of choice to fight console cracks is this Mini-Weld IV Airless Plastic Welder by the Eastwood Company. It comes with a soldering-iron-like welder, two tips, a good selection of plastic welding rod, steel mesh and even a how-to video.

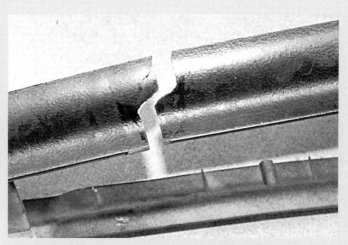

9. This fracture went all the way through one side of the lower section.

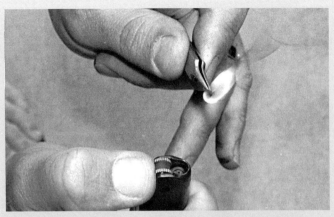

10. To identify what kind of plastic you're dealing with, cut a sliver of material from a hidden section and ignite it with a flame. According to the Mini-Weld manual, the dark, smoky flame we see here means this is ABS plastic——very common in automotive interiors.

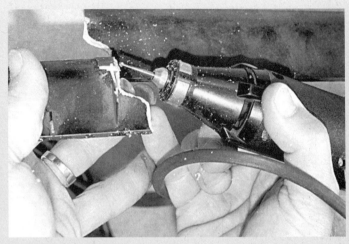

11. With a Dremel tool, bevel both sides of the crack into a V shaped groove.

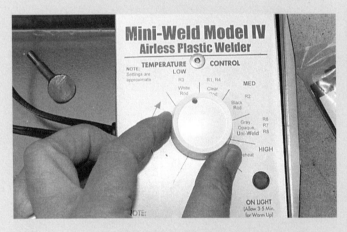

12. Clean the weld area with Eastwood PRE oil-and-silicone remover or equivalent. Then switch the welder knob to the setting for ABS plastic.

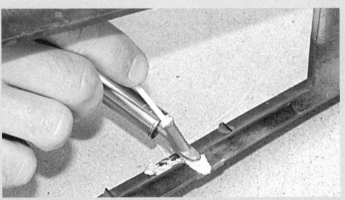

13. When the welder's warmed to operating temperature, slip an ABS rod into the welder tip, lightly press the welder against the plastic and fill the groove with material. It will take a few passes until you get the right touch with the welder. Too much pressure and you'll melt into the console plastic itself; too little pressure and the rod won't stick.

14. Flip the console over and V groove the other side of the crack with the Dremel tool.

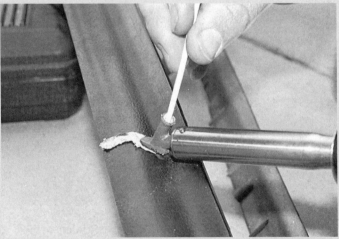

15. Then fill that groove with the ABS rod the same as before.

16. When the welds have cooled, sand them. First use 80-grit, then 180.

17. Clean the area again with PRE or equivalent. Then prime with solvent-based self-etching primer followed by vinyl dye of the correct color for the interior which in this case is black.

18. A mounting boss for the console was also damaged and the broken material was long since gone. This required a different welding procedure utilizing a metal screen and Uni-Weld rod. Clean the area first with PRE or equivalent.

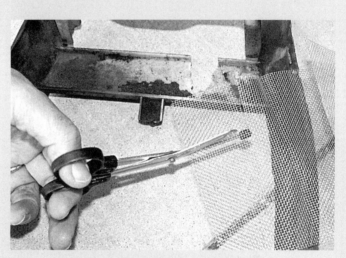

19. Cut the metal screen to fit the damaged area.

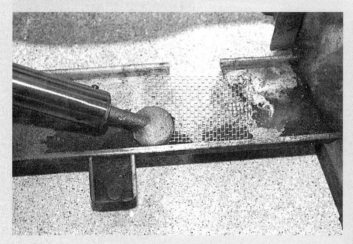

20. With the large, round welding tip, heat the screen while applying gentle pressure until the screen starts to melt into the plastic. This anchors the screen in position.

21. Now melt some Uni-Weld ribbon into the screen and spread it flat with the welding tip.

22. Flip the console over and repeat on the other side of the hole. When the repair has cooled, redrill the hole for the console mounting bolt.

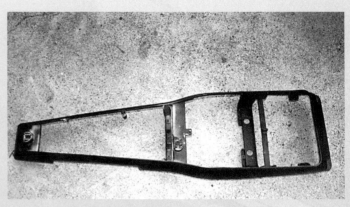

23. Repaired and painted, this lower console section is ready for installation.

24. For a fresh appearance, you can replace the bezels and clear plastic lenses for 1968–69 models separately.

25. Reproduction consoles for 1968–69 Camaros are available from aftermarket sources, either complete or just the main section. With this Classic Industries kit, you can select woodgrain appliqués to match.

26. When it's all done, your console should look as good as the one in this 1969 SS350 convertible.

BODY & TRIM

Chapter 8
Replacing the Windshield

1. Keeping your Camaro's windshield in top form is clearly a battle against the elements.

It's a wonder windshields last as long as they do. Imagine a piece of glass exposed to the elements 365 days a year, bombarded by sand, gravel, bird droppings, tree sap, mass insect suicide, the occasional tungsten-tipped snow-tire stud and assorted other airborne highway flotsam at 65 mph or better. Add to this abuse thousands of wiper passes, some with cracked, torn or missing blades, and your vintage Camaro's windshield looks like it's been doing taxi runs in a war zone.

Minor scratches (ones that won't catch a fingernail) and small sand pits can be polished out with commercially available glass-polishing kits such as that offered by The Eastwood Company. It's a slow and arduous process involving an electric drill, some jeweler's rouge and lots of elbow grease. But sometimes, it can save you the cost of a new windshield.

If your Camaro's front pane is deeply scratched, cracked, stone-chipped or just plain sandblasted, maybe it's time for a replacement. The good news is this is a job you can do at home with just a few specialized tools and a friend to help support and lift off the old windshield and drop in—no, maybe that's the wrong word—place the new one in position.

To give clear access to the windshield, you should first remove the sunvisors, rearview mirror and interior trim moldings from the A-pillars, as well as the wiper arms, radio antenna lead (1970–81 models) and windshield reveal moldings from the outside. Except for the lower windshield molding on 1967–69 Camaros and the upper molding on convertibles, which are retained with Phillips-head screws, you'll need a hooked reveal-molding removal tool to relax the clips retaining the reveal moldings on all other Camaros. This tool, shown in the photos, is available at most tool-

supply and Camaro parts houses.

The windshield (and backlite) is bonded in place and actually forms a part of your Camaro's structure. Breaking that bond requires cutting through the seal, but you'll need more than a garden-variety utility knife. The trick setup is to use piano wire as a cutting tool, the ends of the wire wrapped around two sections of broomstick handle or 3/4" PVC pipe to act as a handle. You first feed one end of the wire through a small hole you'll cut in the rubber seal with an X-Acto or ice pick. Then wrap the wire around the handles, pull the ends of the wire tight and with an assistant on the other end, push the taut wire perpendicular to the glass to break the seal. It takes a lot of muscle to cut the seal.

Aside from the new windshield, other items you'll need to do the installation include a 15-foot roll of new 3M Windo-Weld ribbon sealer, a small can each of brush-on butyl-rubber clear primer and brush-on butyl-rubber adhesive. So let's get started. Getting rid of that old pane is a great way to improve your Camaro's look.

Tools & Supplies Needed
- Windshield glass
- Ribbon sealer
- Butyl primer
- Windshield adhesive
- Piano wire, electrical tape & PVC pipe or molding cutting tool
- Large suction cups with handles
- Windshield reveal molding removal tool
- Glass polishing kit (optional)

2. Loose wiper blade allowed part of arm to repeatedly gouge windshield in a sudden downpour. This scratch isn't too deep and can be polished out. Here we trace the outline of the scratch on the inside of the windshield with a grease pencil to act as a reference during polishing.

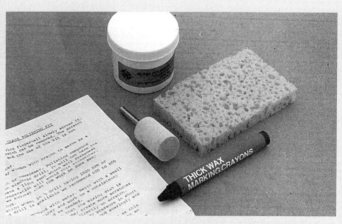

3. Eastwood's glass polishing kit includes special jeweler's compound, polishing wheel and everything needed to remove small scratches.

4. Mix jeweler's with some water and stir into a paste.

5. Mask off the paint and brightwork with newspaper, then wet the window with a sponge.

6. Apply paste compound to scratch, using lots of elbow grease and a low-speed (under 2000 rpm) drill. Keep the glass lubricated with water. Scratch disappeared after polishing for one hour.

7. Windshield is bonded to body with butyl rubber adhesive. To access the seal, remove windshield reveal molding with this hooked tool. Slide tool between glass and underside of reveal molding and move tool along until it hooks on a clip. Pull clip away from car body and gently lift up on molding to disengage it from clip. Repeat for the other 15 or so clips around the windshield. Clean out tree droppings and debris from channel to prevent moisture buildup and rust.

8. Remove the windshield wipers. On 1970–81 models with a windshield antenna, disconnect the lead at the firewall.

9. Also, 1970–81 models have the rearview mirror bonded to the windshield. Remove the mirror from its mount by loosening the set screw with a small Allen wrench. Don't forget to bond a new mirror mount to the new glass. Inside, A-pillar and upper windshield trim moldings should come off for better access.

10. You can cut old butyl rubber seal with piano wire. First pierce seal with an ice pick, feed wire through hole with needle-nose pliers.

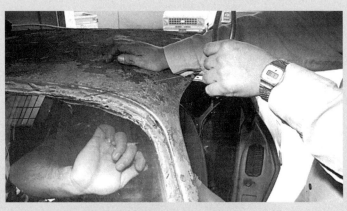

11. Then wrap each end around dowels and cover with electrical tape to make hand grips. With ends held taut, push or pull wire around circumference of windshield. Have a helper support the heavy glass to keep it from falling when seal is broken.

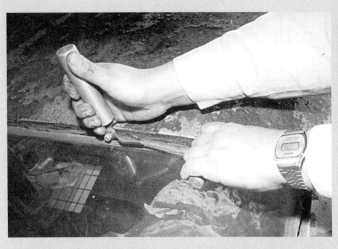

12. Or you can invest in this windshield cutter tool that accomplishes the same thing.

13. You'll need a helper to handle the heavy, unwieldy glass both at removal and installation time. Don't drop it!

14. Scrape off old butyl seal with a putty knife and clean sealing surfaces.

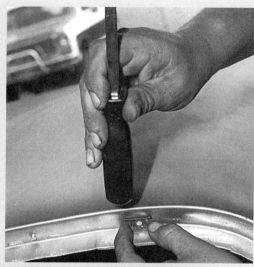

15. Replace damaged or missing windshield reveal molding clips. Some snap onto weld studs; others are retained with screws.

16. Neatly apply clear butyl primer around outer 1/2"of glass.

17. Roll on the ribbon butyl rubber sealer around circumference of windshield. Keep tissue paper on until you're finished moving the sealer into position. Sealer needs to be pliable, so keep room temperature at 70 degrees Fahrenheit or above for best results. On cold days, keep sealer pliable by warming it in microwave on low setting for about a minute.

18. Apply black brush-on adhesive to the windshield opening no more than 15 minutes prior to glass installation.

19. With aid of a helper and suction cups if available, lower new glass into position, centered in opening. Be careful not to pinch any fingers. Once glass is centered, push down on glass with your body weight to help make a positive seal. Shown is the backlite being replaced, however, the procedure is the same for the windshield.

20. Check tightness of seal by pouring water from a large cup. Fix leaks by adding extra butyl sealer. Finally, connect antenna, install reveal moldings, wipers, inside mirror and interior trim pieces and off you go.

Chapter 9
Soft Bumper Repair

1. Soft fascia nose was used on 1978–81 Camaros. Minor damage to urethane outer skin is easily repaired on the car.

Once the National Highway Traffic Safety Administration mandated that cars sold in the U.S. must withstand 5-mph front and 2-1/2-mph rear shunts without damage to the bumpers or body, Camaro design took a decidedly different turn. The year was 1974 and the quick fix was to install huge, ungainly aluminum battering rams perched on giant buggy springs. Needless to say, the bumpers looked like they were adapted from a Checker Marathon taxi, perched awkwardly on the otherwise sensuously curved Camaro front clip. Camaro buyers had to suffer through this "geeky" period until 1978. That year, Chevy figured out how to give both the front and rear ends of the Camaro the bumperless look, soft urethane fascias forever replacing the ungainly aluminum bashers of 1974–77. This is done by fitting a soft urethane skin over a fiberglass form that's bolted to a steel support structure.

Of course Firebirds had this soft fascia setup from the early 1970s, and the grille surround used some of the same technology on the 1970–73 Rally Sport. The seemingly unprotected but energy-absorbing, body-color urethane grille surround and minimalist split bumperettes of the RS made quite a fashion statement.

Car designers love using a urethane-faced nose and tail because they can be easily color-coordinated and seamlessly integrated into the car's overall styling. Also, minor parking-lot altercations are absorbed without drama. But more serious shunts require a lot more repair work than just bolting on a replacement chrome bumper. On 1978-and-later Camaros, repairing nose damage may require removing everything forward of the hood and front fenders. There's a lot of hidden structure to these fascias you can't see.

Minor nicks, gashes and tears in urethane material can be repaired without disassembling your Camaro's nose. All you need is a rotary grinder, putty knife, file, and sandpaper, plus some flexible parts-repair material such as SEM-Weld or equivalent, available in most auto-body and paint supply stores. Though it's really an epoxy-cement-like product, think of SEM-Weld as flexible Bondo; it mixes and is applied in the same manner as body filler. And don't forget that any paint you apply must have flex-agent added to it or it will flake and chip off within weeks.

If the urethane cover was damaged enough that SEM-Weld filler won't restore the shape, chances are that the support structure needs to be looked at. On 1978–81 models, this consists of a fiberglass inner shell that houses the headlamps, park/turn signal lamps and upper grille; a steel inner impact bar and fiberglass facing that gives the "chin" its shape; plus a pair of hefty U-shaped steel brackets, and a crossmember that bolt to the frame horns. Add up the various fasteners and bracketry needed to tie it all together, and needless to say, there's a lot going on behind that pretty face.

If the urethane cover is mangled beyond repair, a new one will set you back some serious coin, but you should be able to find the support pieces, such as, the headlamp/grille inner shell and the bumper impact bar, in a boneyard.

No special tools are required to disassemble and assemble the nose. But you will need a floor jack and a friend to help position and align the assembly while you work the fasteners.

Tools & Supplies Needed
- Floor jack
- Regular hand tools
- SEM Weld (small repairs)
- Rotary grinder (small repairs)
- Sandpaper (180- and 400-grit)
- Flexible primer

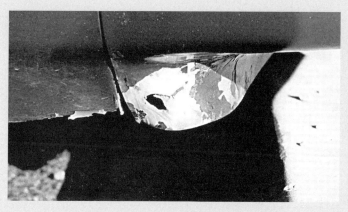

2. Biggest problem with integrated spoiler on soft front fascia is damage from whacking curbs, speed bumps and parking-lot dividers.

3. Support the front end underneath the front fascia with a floor jack cushioned by a wooden block before unbolting anything. Grille, headlamps and parking lamps can be left in place if desired. Remove attaching screws and stud nuts; there's six at each fender, one at bottom of hood latch support, four behind radiator support and four (two from above and two from below) at impact bar.

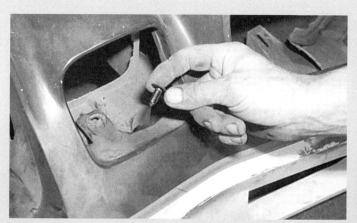

4. Once removed from car, place fascia on cardboard to prevent scratching. Pry out this plastic rivet from each parking lamp cavity before separating urethane cover from its fiberglass support.

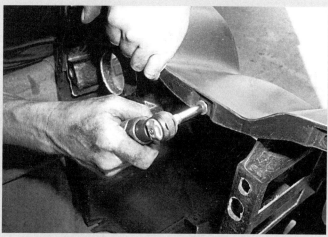

5. Unbolt hex screws retaining cover to support.

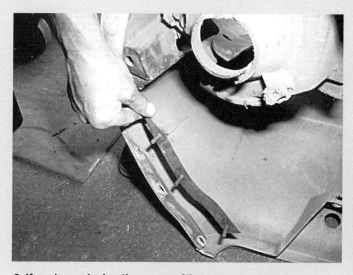

6. If you're replacing the cover with a new one, transfer hardware such as these retainer strips to the replacement piece. You need these to bolt the cover to each lower front fender.

7. Inspect headlamp aiming/mounting hardware and replace broken plastic pieces and bent or stripped screws.

8. Damaged fiberglass support struts inside headlamp cavity can prevent proper operation/aiming of headlamps.

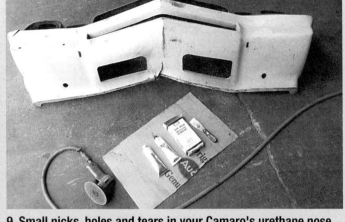

9. Small nicks, holes and tears in your Camaro's urethane nose cover can be repaired with SEM-Weld flexible parts repair material or equivalent, saving you the cost and hassle of installing a new replacement. Though the repair can be performed on-car, we used a spare cover here for illustrative purposes.

10. Bevel edges on repair area about 1-2" with rotary sander to help adhesion of repair material. Go slowly because cover material is much softer than steel! Then featheredge the area with 180-grit sandpaper and blow clean. Wash off with soap and water followed by wax, grease and silicone remover such as Pre-Kleano.

11. Squeeze out equal parts of plastic filler and catalyst, and mix according to manufacturer directions. SEM-Weld sets up in roughly 10 minutes, depending on temperature and humidity.

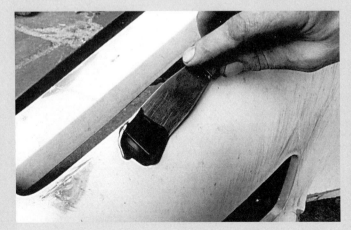

12. Apply filler with a putty knife or flexible squeegee using even strokes. Build it up higher than surrounding urethane to allow for shrinkage.

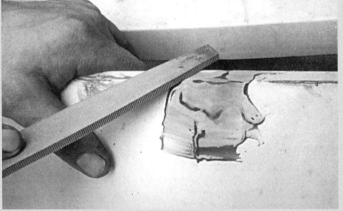

13. Allow to dry for 30 minutes, then shape repair with a medium-fine file, dual-action sander or block sander with 180-grit paper.

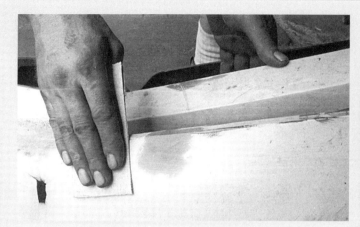

14. Finish sanding with 400-grit paper. Use extreme care to follow character lines.

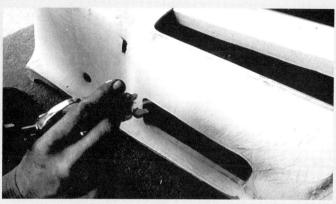

15. Apply flexible primer. When dry, scuff-sand and check for any high or low spots. If OK, prime again, clean area you plan to paint with Prep-Sol, then spray on the color coat containing a flex-agent.

16. Insert replacement support inside urethane cover, bolt the two together and set them aside for now.

17. If damaged, bumper impact bar and cushion can be removed as a unit. Hefty steel impact bar will survive all but the most severe shunts.

18. Four large hex nuts for impact-bar are accessed from inside these two U-shaped brackets. Brackets are energy-absorbing and may be "collapsed" after a collision.

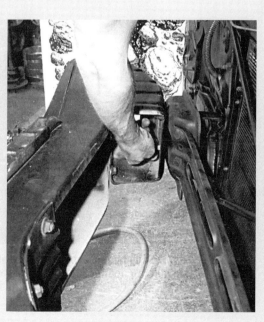

19. Front-ender may also tweak hood-latch mechanism and support. Remove it to get to impact-bar supports and frame brackets. Before removing latch-mechanism bolts, mark position of eccentric holes to aid assembly.

20. Stout, steel impact-bar brackets attach to frame horns. If either bracket is bent, check car's subframe dimensionally on a jig.

21. If impact-bar brackets are damage-free, leave them alone to preserve adjustments. Use bubble level to check vertical alignment of brackets on impact-bar crossmember.

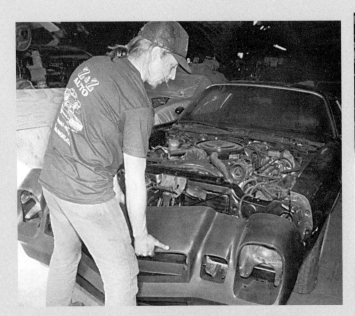

22. After installing impact-bar assembly and hood latch, get some help mounting the unwieldy soft fascia and support assembly. Place a floor jack underneath and start urethane cover-to-body hex screws and stud nuts by hand. Then make the attachments to the impact bar and hood-latch support.

23. Don't tighten any cover hex screws until you've checked nose-to-body alignment. If everything is straight, tighten nose attaching hardware and reinstall grille, headlamps and park/turn-signal lamps, if removed. Now your Camaro's ready to show its handsome face to the world again.

Chapter 10

Vinyl Top Repair

1. Hundreds of thousands of Camaros were originally built with vinyl tops, like this 1970 Sport Coupe here. The duct tape covering tears in this car's vinyl top, however, were an owner-installed accessory.

It wasn't all that long ago that high automotive fashion for coupes and sedans of all varieties included a vinyl roof covering. "Today's Chevrolet" of the late 1960s and early 1970s quite often was fitted with a vinyl roof.

If you're restoring a Camaro to factory-original condition and the body and trim tag says that the car rolled off the assembly line with a vinyl top, you'll enjoy greater appreciation and resale value if you keep the vinyl roof, even if current styling trends say otherwise. Or reinstall the top if some former owner had removed it.

On most Camaros, the vinyl-coated fabric roof cover is made up from three dielectrically bonded sections. At the factory, these are glued to the roof with a non-staining nitrile adhesive, with the edges retained to the window aperatures with trim clips and drive nails. At the drip rails, it's folded under, glued and kept in place with the weatherstripping and drip moldings. At the bottom of the C-pillar and tulip panel, it's retained with more glue, trim clips and drive nails. The whole operation is not unlike installing wall-to-wall carpet.

As with any 20-to-30-year-old car, years of exposure to the elements fades, dries out and cracks the vinyl. And because most Camaros were never painted or ELPO-dipped in rust-preventive primer in the roof area, any break in the vinyl can exposc bare, unpainted metal to moisture. Once rust gets a foothold, it can spread quickly to other unprotected areas and severely compromise the structural integrity of your car. You can't just bolt on a new roof.

You can usually spot a Camaro with roof rust, even if the vinyl top is cosmetically sound. Look for raised dimples or bubbles in the vinyl that crunch when you push on them. If you find a preponderance of bubbles, the best strategy is to strip off the vinyl and have the rust sections repaired. Then once you've restored the roof to good metal, use a good self-etching primer and recover with a new top.

To replace the vinyl top with a new covering, it is necessary to remove the reveal moldings for the windshield and backlite, as well as the drip moldings (where applicable), window weatherstripping, and quarter panel and tulip-panel trim moldings. You'll want to cover the window glass with tape to avoid scratching or dripping glue on it. And installation will go much easier if you pull out the nails for the windshield and backlite reveal-molding clips. A stout putty knife is excellent for working loose the old top; for stubborn sections, use a heat gun or hair dryer to loosen the adhesive bond.

With lots of patience and elbow grease, you can install a new vinyl top in an afternoon.

Tools & Supplies Needed

- Spray contact adhesive
- Masking tape
- Chalk
- Scissors
- Tack-puller
- Putty knife
- Single-edge razor
- Windshield reveal-molding removal tool

2. If you suspect your Camaro's vinyl top was already replaced once, make sure it was done right. Here, a new "quickie" top was installed over existing roof rust. Look for the telltale signs of rust "bubbles" forming underneath.

3. What looks like corn flakes under that fabric tear used to be Chevy steel.

4. Reveal moldings are removed with a special tool (see page 41, photo 7 in the windshield replacement section) available at most automotive tool stores and mail-order GM parts outlets. Slide tool between the glass and molding and drag hooked end along until you contact a reveal-molding clip. Then pull clip away from roof slightly to spring molding loose. Repeat for each clip around windshield and backlite.

5. Plastic clips retain bright molding at base of C-pillar and tulip panel. Use a tack puller to carefully pry up molding. Use new plastic clips for installation.

6. After removing the roof weatherstripping and moldings, work old vinyl cover loose with a putty knife while pulling with your free hand.

7. After old vinyl cover is removed, check roof for rust. If the painted surface is fine, leave it alone. More times than not, however, there is some light corrosion which should be removed with phosphatizing jelly or sanding. Sandblast severely rusted areas. If you find any perforations or holes, a new roof section from a donor car needs to be welded in. Don't leave any bare metal. Apply self-etching primer before recovering the roof.

8. Before you get out that glue, make a dry run. Mark roof centerline and position of fabric seams onto masking tape strips on the windsheld and backlite. This aids alignment later on because once the adhesive is applied, wiggle room for final adjustments is limited.

9. Inspect top for defects or tears, then spread it out upside down and apply aerosol contact adhesive.

10. Mask the windows and spray contact adhesive on the roof. With an assistant, carefully align the top with the marks made earlier and drop it in place. Keep the top slightly taut to avoid wrinkles. Avoid pressing the top down firmly so it can be moved around if necessary for alignment.

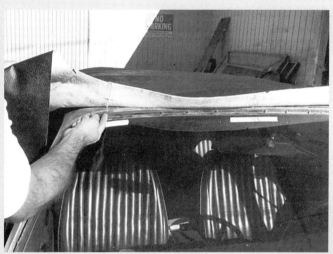

11. Align top seams with the marks you had made on windshield and backlite earlier.

12. Stretch corners tight to work out wrinkles and folds.

13. Cut small radial slits in the fabric to "relieve" the fabric and prevent curling around the radius of sharp corners.

14. Trace window openings with chalk, then trim off excess leaving a 3/4" overlap to fold into window openings.

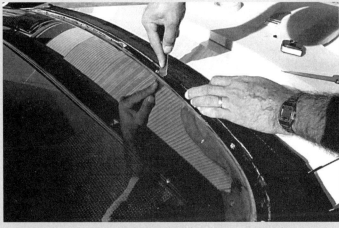

15. Press overlapping fabric into window openings and around weld studs for reveal molding clips using a small putty knife.

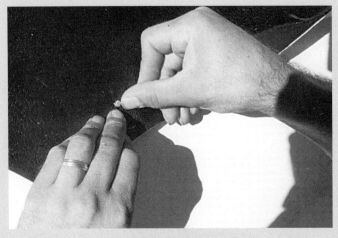

16. Cut a small slit for each weld stud, then stretch new top over nail head. This helps anchor top in position and prevents curling years later.

17. Reinstall reveal-molding clips on their weld studs, then press back on stainless-steel reveal moldings.

18. Use plenty of contact adhesive to wrap the top tightly into the weatherstripping channels in the side-window openings, then install door window weatherstripping and drip moldings (where applicable). Now you can put away the duct tape because your Camaro's vinyl top is ready for many years of sun and fun.

1. A Z28 just doesn't look like a Z28 when its stripes are missing.

Chapter 11

Restoring Z28 Runway Stripes

When today's performance models need a little visual pizzazz, the factory applies body graphics in the form of adhesive-backed vinyl appliqués. But there was a time when Detroit's finest muscle cars roared off the assembly line with really cool graphics painted on by UAW brothers. From 1967 to 1973, the bold "runway" stripes running down the hood and decklid of the legendary Camaro Z28 were sprayed on. Unlike the tape stripes and huge vinyl appliqués that would be used on Z28s from 1974 and on, given proper care, these painted stripes would last as long as the paint on the rest of the car. Super Sport and Rally Sport Camaros also got treated to their own special paint stripes.

Problem was, when it came time to repaint or restore the car, finding an original car with the same stripes in order to take measurements was difficult at best. Even then, while it was easy to find reference points for the straight sections, getting those compound curves right was next to impossible.

Today you can buy a stencil kit for the exact year and model of Camaro you're working on. The kits take all the guesswork out of where the stripes go and handle the toughest curves with ease. You still have to be careful about masking and surface prep, but where to apply paint is no longer a question.

We contacted Ralph Greinke Jr. of Stencils & Stripes Unlimited in the Chicago suburb of Park Ridge, Illinois, for some advice on applying stripes to a pair of 1973 Z28s undergoing restoration. His high-quality stencil kits are sold direct or through most of the mail-order Camaro parts outlets across the U.S.

The kits come with adhesive-backed vinyl stencils for the front, rear, and curvy parts of the stripes, a roll of 9/32" tape to connect the straight sections, a squeegee to work out air bubbles, and detailed instructions giving measurements from key reference points. In addition, you'll need some masking tape, masking paper (our painter used large plastic dry-

Tools & Supplies Needed

- Stencil kit
- Squeegee
- Masking tape
- Masking paper or plastic sheeting
- Tape measure
- Squirt bottle
- Dishwashing liquid and water
- Hand tools for removing badges and trim

cleaning bags), a tape measure, a spray bottle filled with a mild, soapy-water solution (Joy dishwashing liquid works well), plus all the normal paint-prep paraphernalia.

Each stencil looks like a three-layer sandwich. It consists of a paper-like premask on top which sometimes has printed instructions on it like RIGHT SIDE (passenger side) or LEFT SIDE (driver side). The actual adhesive-backed, die-cut vinyl stencil is in the middle, and a heavier plastic backing material is on the bottom. Sometimes separating these layers can be tedious, so have patience and don't try to pull off one layer too quickly—the vinyl stencil could stretch, tear or become otherwise damaged.

Never apply the stencils and paint the stripes over a fresh paint job that hasn't cured yet. Fresh paint releases solvents as it is curing and if these are trapped under the stencils, it may cause the paint to separate and lift when the stencils are removed. Also, make sure the surface to be painted is squeaky clean—no wax, polish, grease, dust or dirt. If in doubt, use a tack rag prior to applying paint.

One minor issue; there's controversy these days about "over-restoring" to a level of craftsmanship greater than that originally bestowed on these mass-produced cars. Specifically, as it relates to runway stripes, the thoroughness of the way the stripes were cut in at the leading edges of the hood, trunk, trailing edges of the header panel, and tulip panel seems to vary greatly from car to car. If you want a real neat-looking job, then mask and cut these areas in first before painting the large horizontal surfaces. Or if you want that factory-original look, just mask the horizontal surfaces and let the paint fall where it may in the gaps between these panels. I prefer the former.

Whichever path you take, don't rush the job. The stencils are quality pieces, and if applied correctly they'll help you create original-quality factory stripes for your Z28 that'll look good for years and years to come.

2. Add runway stripes and this 1970 Z28 is recognizable for the great musclecar it is.

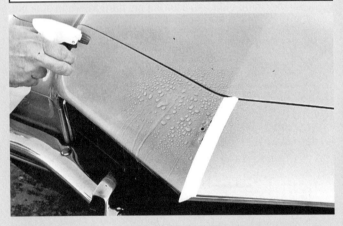

3. Before applying stencils, wipe down the car and make sure it's completely free of dirt, dust, old wax and any contaminants. Mark the center of the header panel with masking tape; it's easy to find because there's a ridge there. Then, wet down the area with a mild solution of dishwashing soap and water. Applying this spray helps you make fine adjustments aligning the stencil, even after the adhesive is stuck to the body, and makes elimination of trapped air bubbles easier later on with a squeegee.

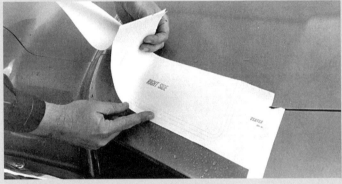

4. Header-panel stencil is in two pieces, clearly marked RIGHT SIDE and LEFT SIDE. Align stencil's inboard edge with tape marking the header-panel center line and align the small 1/16" notches cut into sides of the stencil with the gap between the header panel and hood. When aligned perfectly, there's 2.5" between the center line and inboard edge of the first stripe cutout on 1970–73 models. If everything's OK, pull off the plastic backing and stick the stencil in place using a squeegee.

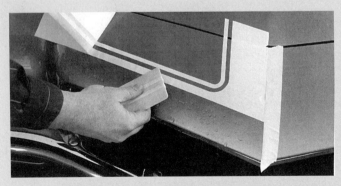

5. Now carefully peel off the paper premask top layer along with center portions of the vinyl stencil that will receive the paint stripes. Start at one corner and pull slowly and steadily so as not to damage the vinyl. If a section lifts as you remove the premask, gently work the vinyl stencil back into place with the squeegee. The thin 1/4" stripes will give you the most trouble.

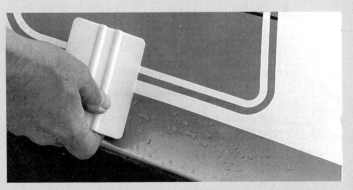

6. After using the squeegee to remove all of the soapy water from underneath the vinyl stencil, it'll be stuck in place. If you want to mask off the gap between the hood and header panel (optional), open the hood and do it before you get too far along or you'll tear the stencil trying to move it. Repeat these steps for applying the driver-side stencil to the opposite side of the header panel.

7. Move to the rear of the hood, find the center, and mark it with masking tape. On 1970–73 models, the hood is 58" wide at the rear, so the tape is placed at 29". Spray the hood with soapy solution.

8. Position the rear hood stencils against the tape and peel off the heavy plastic backing. Squeegee out excess moisture so the stencil adhesive sticks to the hood.

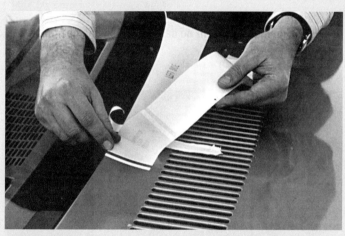

9. Peel off top paper premask, being careful to lift off only stripe sections that are to receive paint. Starting at one end, anchor sections that must stick to the body with a free finger or two.

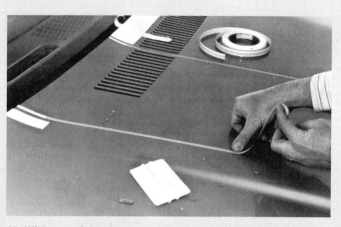

10. With a straightedge, connect the stencil at the rear of the hood with the one at the header panel using the adhesive-backed 9/32" "pin-stripe" tape provided in the kit. On the 1970–73 Camaro runway stripes you'll be painting on the hood taper wider front-to-back, ending up at 16-3/8" width at the windshield.

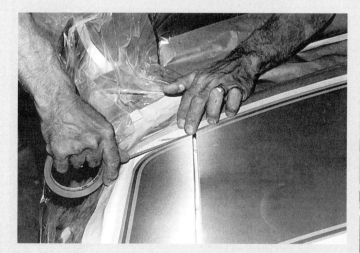

11. Run the tape forward to the header-panel stencil. This painter has already cut in the hood-to-header panel gap with color coat.

12. Mask off the fenders with large sheets of masking paper available from auto paint supply stores.

13. Or you can wrap the fenders, windshield and nose with large plastic dry-cleaner bags. Don't forget to tape inside the cowl vents to prevent overspray from hitting the firewall.

14. The 1970–73 nose is now stenciled, taped, masked and ready for paint.

15. At the rear, find the center of the tulip panel at the backlite. On 1970–73 models, this is 45", so we put masking tape at 22.5".

16. Also find the center of the rear spoiler or rear edge of the trunk lid (on 1972–73 models without the optional D80 spoiler). The easiest way to do this is to bisect the center of the rear lock cylinder and mark with masking tape. Aligned correctly, the inboard edge of the first thin stripe will be 3-11/16" from this center line. Also, there are slight variations to the rear edge of the stripes depending on model year. The 1970 low spoiler and 1973 high spoiler have stripes with radiused ends; 1971–72 models have straight ends that butt at the bottom edge of the spoiler. See your kit instructions for further details.

17. Spray the rear panel with soapy water and peel the heavy plastic backing off the stencil. The 6" long slot cut into the middle of the stencil should be at the top. Apply the adhesive-backed stencil and squeegee in place.

18. Fold the stencil over the top of the spoiler (unless your 1972–73 Z28 doesn't have one) and carefully peel off the paper premask. Squeegee again.

19. Apply stencil to one side of the spoiler, then to the other side.

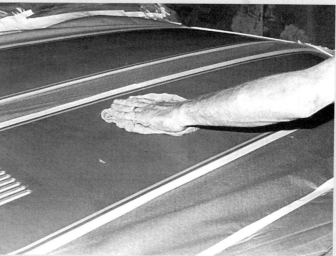

20. Unlike the hood stripes, the decklid stripes keep a constant width front to back of 14-1/2", each spaced 4" from the center line. Continue the tape stripes straight forward to the backlite and mask the rear quarters, rear window, roof and rear of car.

21. Allow the stencils to dry for roughly one hour. They must be completely free of moisture or soap residue before applying paint. Wipe the surfaces to be painted with a tack rag.

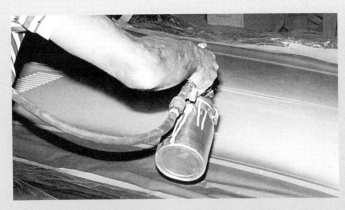

22. When applying succeeding coats of paint, allow time to dry in between. If using enamel, the stencil can be lifted off as soon as the color has set. With synthetic enamels, Stencils & Stripes Unlimited recommends waiting about an hour before removing the stencil. And with lacquer, it's best to either remove the stencil immediately after painting to avoid "bridging" or ragged edges, or let the whole car—body, masking and stencils—dry completely beforehand.

23. Here's a set of finished stripes on a 1973 Z28 Rally Sport. Notice how these stripes start farther forward on the header panel than non-RS Z28s.

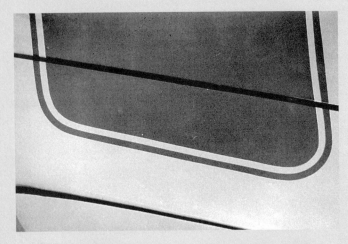

24. Stencil kit gives proper radius to forward ends of hood stripes.

25. Homemade hood stripes on this 1970 Z28 are incorrect. The forward edges are too far forward on the header panel and the radiuses are too abrupt. Save yourself the grief and get the stencil kit.

26. Runway stripes on the decklid and rear spoiler leave the Z28 signature for all to see.

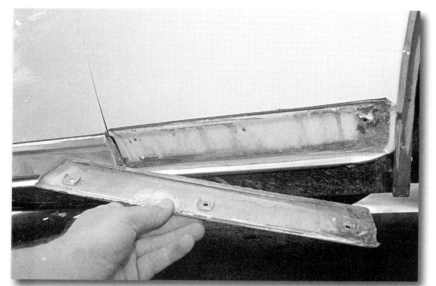

1. Remove three Phillips-head screws, and the front-fender portion of the lower body-side molding should lift right off. Note the buildup of dirt and debris behind the molding that can lead to corrosion.

Chapter 12

Restoring Brightwork

One of the major factors that sets a Camaro apart from its more pedestrian Nova and Malibu siblings is style. Even though the two Chevrolet sedans share many a common suspension, brake, electrical, and driveline part with Camaro, the seductively shaped coupe has it all over them in the product-lust department.

When it comes to maximizing curb appeal, think of your Camaro's exterior as a total fashion statement. In a metaphorical sense, the paintwork is the suit; wheels and tires, the shoes; and the car's brightwork its jewelry. If any of the three elements isn't up to snuff, the car just lacks that certain something. Apply nail paint, wheels, and chrome and suddenly, your Camaro is way more than the sum of its parts.

Aside from badges and bumpers, most of the bright trim on early Camaros is polished aluminum—which is a good-news, bad-news proposition. The good news is aluminum never rusts. The bad news is it pits rather easily. On a 30-something-year-old Camaro such as our 1967 Rally Sport project car, the lower body side moldings often take a beating from road debris, the elements, and sometimes, paint overspray.

To restore brilliance, your choices are either polishing them or replacing them with aftermarket pieces (GM no longer supplies these moldings). In either case, the old moldings have to be removed. This is a worthwhile endeavor regardless, because moisture and debris tend to accumulate behind the moldings, sometimes leading to corrosion.

Most moldings have exposed screws and are easy to deal with. But sometimes the fasteners are hidden inside door jambs or behind panels. Check the appropriate *Assembly Manual* or *Fisher Body Manual* for your year of Camaro. On 1967–68 Camaros, the deluxe lower body side moldings are retained to the doors with clips fastened by hex nuts from inside the doors. The only way to remove the clips is to first remove the door trim panel.

Once removed, you can inspect the trim more closely to see if it can be cleaned up, polished and restored to tip-top shape or is in need of replacement. We split the difference on our project Rally Sport (RS), electing to install new body side moldings from D&R Classic Automotive on one side and polishing the originals with a kit from the Eastwood Company on the other. If your car's moldings aren't too far gone, polishing should do the trick and you'll save hundreds of dollars in the process. Ours were seriously pitted, however, and we eventually installed new D&R polished aluminum deluxe trim moldings on both sides, restoring the car's appearance to like-new.

2. Check around door jambs for hidden screws.

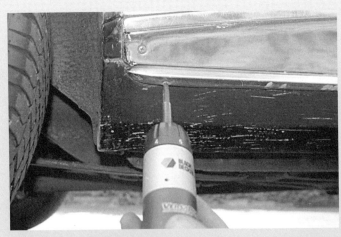

3. Long spear-shaped rocker molding is retained at each end with a single Phillips-head screw.

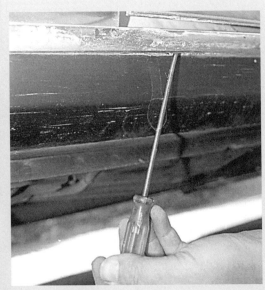

4. Rocker molding "hangs" on mounting bracket. Gently pry outward on lower edges to pop it loose from car.

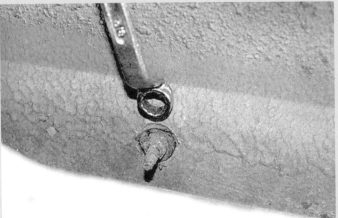

5. Clips for lower body side moldings are bolted inside door. To access hex nuts, remove door trim panel. Use lots of WD-40 or equivalent to ease removal of nuts from studs on clips.

6. If paint is otherwise in good shape, minor rust behind moldings can be neutralized with Neutra Rust or equivalent.

7. The Eastwood Company offers a complete polishing kit which includes 6" buffing wheels, compounds and instructions to brighten just about any kind of brightwork on your Camaro. Polished aluminum lower body-side molding shown here was badly pitted.

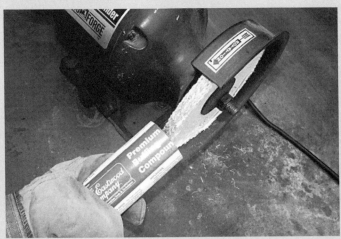

8. Install buffing wheel on 1/2-horsepower electric grinder. Turn on grinder and work compound into wheel.

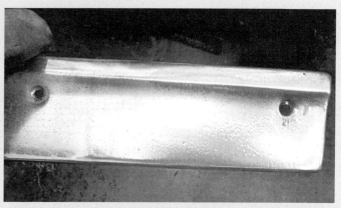

9. Wearing protective gloves, a breathing mask and eyewear, polish the trim using steady pressure and even strokes. Follow the directions in the instructions because the type of polishing wheels and compounds used varies with the metal being buffed. Always keep the work perpendicular to the buffing wheel.

10. After about an hour of buffing this polished, aluminum body side molding, it still had visible pits, so we elected to go with new pieces instead. But in other situations, the Eastwood kit can deliver like-new brilliance.

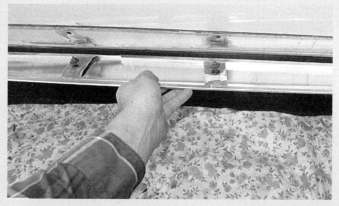

11. In some cases, it's necessary to transfer attaching hardware from old moldings to new ones. For these door moldings, slide clips to center and out through this slot.

12. Slide the clips in the grooves so they align with the holes in the body.

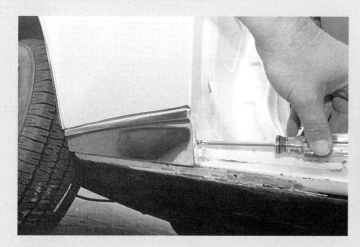

13. Before installing moldings, clean the paintwork with rubbing compound as a further inhibitor to rust.

14. New chrome from D&R Automotive really wakes up the appearance and gives this '67 Camaro a clean, well-dressed look. The reproduction pieces fit well, too.

Chapter 13
Door Glass Replacement & Adjustment

1. If your Camaro's frameless door glass isn't adjusted properly, wind and water leaks will be the order of the day. Sagging door hinges and decomposed weatherstripping don't help either.

The frameless door glass used in your Camaro's side windows looks sporty, but its design makes it difficult to get a weather-tight seal. Except for 1967 models that had a separate pivoting vent window and vertical channel, Camaro side glass is supported only along its bottom edge. So unless the window weatherstrip is compliant and intact and the door glass is adjusted properly, there are many opportunities for wind and water to enter the cabin.

Inspect the rubber weatherseal that runs along the door opening from A-pillar to roof to B-pillar. If it is cracked, torn or dried out, the weatherstrip must be replaced before attempting any side-window adjustments. Also, with the window rolled down on 1968–81 models, inspect the two postage-stamp-sized stabilizers on the inboard side of the glass. These have a felt covering that when worn through will cause the glass to become scratched as it is rolled up and down. On 1967 Camaros, check the condition of the felt runner on the rear edge of the vent window support.

If you find minor scratches that won't catch a fingernail, these can usually be removed with commercially available glass polishing kits, such as the kit from The Eastwood Company. Deeply scratched glass, as well as discolored or broken glass, requires replacement. If you're real serious about using only original Libby Owens Ford date-coded glass, good luck, because most used side glass you'll find will be scratched as well.

On 1968–81 models, there are no less than six different adjustments that can be performed to restore a weather-tight seal. To adjust or replace door glass, you must first remove the interior trim panel. The only tricky trim item is the window-winder handle; it's retained with a small, horseshoe clip that's virtually impossible to remove without a

Tools & Supplies Needed
- Socket set (3/8" drive)
- Phillips-head screwdriver
- Tack-puller
- Window crank horseshoe-clip removal tool
- Putty knife
- Needle-nose pliers
- Snap-On S9610 or equivalent bellcrank nut removal tool
- Lubriplate or other white grease

commercially available clip-removal tool. Get the tool, and the rest is removable with a putty knife, Phillips screwdriver, needle-nose pliers and other common handtools.

If the Camaro you're working on is original, the trim panels are probably constructed of vinyl-covered hardboard. When prying the hardboard free of the door, find each retaining clip and give support under the clip as you pop it loose to prevent the clip from tearing through the hardboard. Once all fasteners are removed, the trim panel lifts up and clear of the door. Behind the trim panel (if your Camaro is original or the door's never been apart) is a tar paper water shield attached to the door with tape and dumdum. If damaged, you'll need to replace the water shield later on with a die-cut aftermarket replacement or heavy sheet plastic wrap such as Visqueen. Without the water shield, your Camaro's interior trim panel may suffer water damage when it rains.

Glass is both heavy and fragile. If you're replacing the glass, you'll be working through access holes cut in the inner door panel. Support under the glass as you remove its fasteners, and be careful to avoid getting a finger caught between the glass and jagged sheet metal. And don't drop it. Side windows are made from tempered glass and can shatter into hundreds, maybe thousands, of small, non-jagged pieces.

When you buy new glass it comes without the rollers, washers, bearings stops and bellcranks that bolt to the lower part of the glass. You'll have to transfer them over from the old panes. These are retained to the glass with special nuts that have two 1/8" holes 180 degrees apart; a special 2-pin nut removal/installation tool, Snap-On S9610 or equivalent, is required for the job (see photo 24 on page 67). Point-type snap-ring pliers don't really have the leverage to break the nuts loose. Or if you're on good terms with the local glass shop, have them

transfer the hardware for you. A good, used side window will likely have the hardware you need already attached to it, if you can find one.

Always lay glass on a surface protected with large towels or pieces of cardboard to prevent scratching. Push comes to shove, carefully tap the 2-hole nuts loose with a pin-punch and hammer. Be careful. It doesn't take much of a hit to shatter tempered glass into little pieces.

Remember, go slowly and be methodical. Make only one adjustment at a time, then check the fit of the glass in the door opening. By the numbers, the adjustments are: (1) inboard-outboard, (2) fore-aft tilt, (3) winder effort, (4) rotation, (5) up-travel stops and (6) down-travel stop.

2. No amount of door glass adjustments will keep the elements out, however, if your Camaro's side-window weatherstripping isn't pliant.

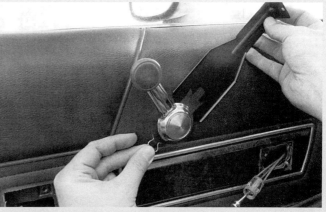

3. One of two special tools you'll need to replace side glass is this horseshoe-clip removing tool. You'll never get the window cranks off without it.

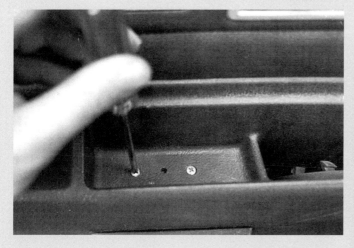

4. You must remove the door trim panel to access the glass. Note that some screws may be hidden inside door pulls.

5. Remove the screws for the armrest and unscrew the door lock knob.

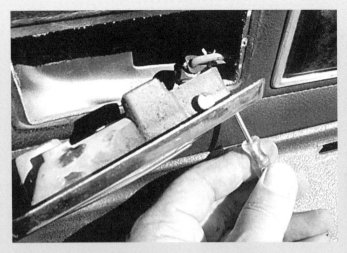

6. Disengage circlip from inside door latch pull rod.

7. Sight down the front and rear edges of the trim panel and find the two or three retaining clips on each side. To avoid tearing the fragile hardboard backing to the trim panel during removal, lever with a tack puller directly beneath clips.

8. These small metal clips are easily torn from their pockets in the hardboard trim panel. When hardboard is torn away, trim panel won't fit tight on door.

9. Also easily damaged are these "Christmas tree" plastic clips. New ones are available at auto supply stores.

10. Trim panel lifts straight up and off hangers at beltline.

11. While trim panel is off, it's a good time to check the condition of the inboard door felt. Cracked and brittle felt can't wipe condensation from inside window when it's rolled down, and should be replaced.

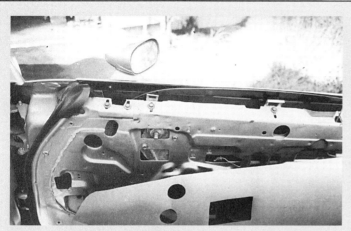

12. Tar paper water seal keeps moisture from warping and mildewing trim-panel backing. If it's damaged or missing, install a new one at assembly time.

13. If you're removing the door glass, first remove the outer window felt because it gets in the way. You may need an offset screwdriver to get at some of the screws. Some outer felts may be held on with plastic rivets; pull these out with needle-nose pliers.

14. Two stabilizers atop door have felt-covered pads that can be adjusted to regulate winder effort. Unbolt them for clearance if you're replacing the glass.

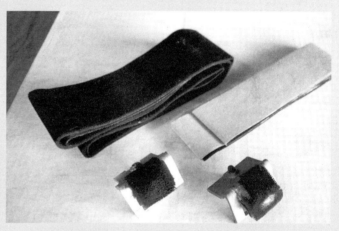

15. Stabilizer at lower right has worn through felt pad, causing deep scratches in door glass. Either replace stabilizer or if not available, cover with new felt material shown above.

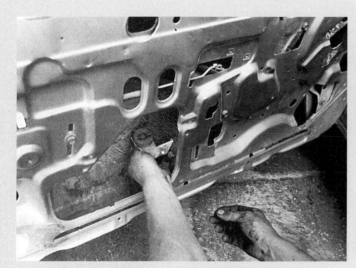

16. Lower stop is adjustable on 1967 and 1970–81 models. Remove it on 1970–81 Camaros to aid access to glass.

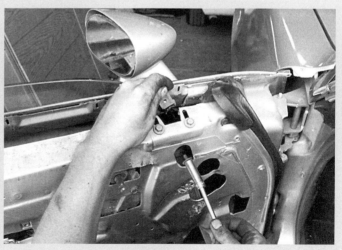

17. To remove glass, crank window to 3/4 position. Remove front upper stop.

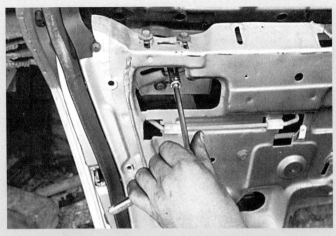

18. Then remove rear upper stop. Incidentally, the front and rear upper stop bolts are in slotted channels and control window height adjustment to roof weatherstrip.

19. Down below, remove the front lower sash channel nut...

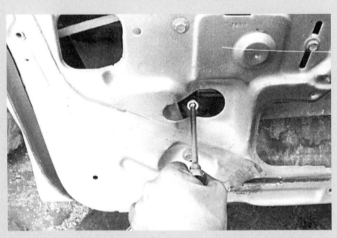

20. ...then unbolt the rear lower sash channel nut. Support under the glass now or it will fall to the bottom of the door.

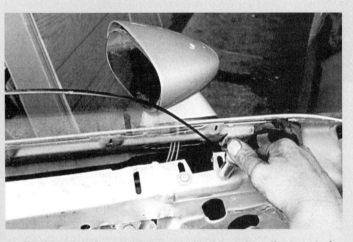

21. To aid removal, you may want to back out the adjustment of the front and rear upper guide bolts that control in-out tilt adjustment.

22. Carefully lift the old glass up and out.

23. Most new glass comes without attaching hardware, rollers and so on. To swap hardware, lay the glass on a flat, padded surface. Some hardware attaches with common hex bolts.

24. The forward bellcrank assembly is retained to the glass with special 2-hole nuts. To transfer the bellcrank to the new glass, this homemade 2-prong tool or Snap-On S9610 will do the job without jeopardizing the glass.

25. Be sure to remember the order of washers as you transfer the stops, rollers and bellcranks to the new window. Lubricate rollers with Lubriplate or equivalent. If any are broken or binding, or if the window made a "clicking" sound when rolling up or down, now is the time to replace them. New replacements can be obtained from Camaro parts suppliers.

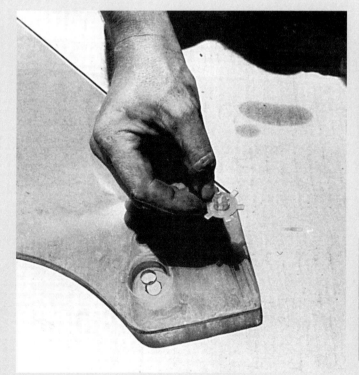

26. This star-shaped plastic guide helps keep the glass from rubbing in the track. Pry it loose with a screwdriver and snap it into the new glass.

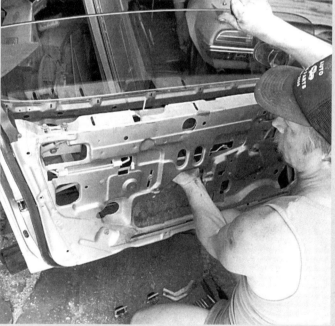

27. While supporting from underneath, carefully lower the new glass into position. Bolt the front and rear sash-channel nuts to the glass and install the lower stop/rubber bumper. Adjust in-out, up-down and winder effort, as described earlier.

Chapter 14

Replacing Door & Side Glass Weatherstripping

1. Worn weatherstripping lets in water and dirt. Here two dried-up old sections of roof-rail weatherstripping were actually spliced together, and not very well at that.

The weatherstripping around the windows, doors, hood and trunk of your Camaro performs the key task of keeping the great outdoors out, and basic goodness in. The principle is simple enough: stuff some sponge rubber into the gaps and cracks between panels. And where necessary, form some channels in the rubber to route whatever you don't want getting in to your Camaro and away from where you don't want it to go, preventing soggy carpets, door panels and seats.

Sponge rubber, however, doesn't last forever. Oil turns it to mush. Sun converts it to so much dust. Extreme temperatures harden it. Constant friction with sliding panels tears it apart. Repeated compression crushes it. Time shrinks it. After 20 or 30 years of holding a thin line between Mother Nature and your Camaro's softer side, the old weatherstripping needs to go to rubber heaven and new stuff installed.

Make a visual check of the rubber for cracks, tears, and obvious decomposition. Obvious symptoms of weatherstripping distress are water leaks and wind whistles. If you can't ride through a drive-through car wash without getting a bath, or if your Camaro sounds like a whistling tea kettle running down the road when the windows are up, chances are the weatherstrips in question are not sealing properly.

Poor sealing, however, is sometimes hard to pinpoint. Try taking a sheet of copier or typing paper, placing it over the weatherstripping in question and closing the door, window, trunk or whatever. If the seal is tight, you should be able to pull the paper through with moderate force. If the paper slips through with ease, the weatherstripping isn't sealing properly. Another way to check for weathertightness is with chalk. Apply soft chalk to the weatherstrip sealing surface on the body, then close the door or trunk lid and open it again.

Tools & Supplies Needed
- Flat-blade screwdriver
- Phillips-head screwdriver
- Tack puller
- Putty knife
- Needle-nose pliers
- 3M Weatherstrip adhesive (black) or equivalent
- Weatherstrip kit

Check for a uniform coating of chalk on the weatherstrip. Any gaps indicate possible leakage paths.

Weatherstripping designed to fit the specific year and model of your Camaro is available from GM dealers (late models only) or the Camaro parts aftermarket. I recommend buying weatherstripping in sets. For one thing, if one weather seal is starting to decompose, the others can't be far behind. And fresh rubber sealing is an important part of any restoration. Why bother with shiny new paint and interior fabric if the rubber is dried out and cracked? Also, you'll save money by buying a complete set of weather seals compared to buying each one individually. These generally include door, roof-rail or pillar-post seals, inner and outer window seals (fuzzies), trunk and cowl seals, and on 1967–69 models, vertical and U-shaped quarter-window seals. On 1967 models, you may also want to replace the pivoting front vent-window seals, about $50 a pair. Prepare to spend several hundred dollars for a complete set of weather seals for coupes. Add even more for '67–'69 convertibles and '78–'81 T-tops.

As you shop the aftermarket for replacement weather seals, you'll find most Camaro parts outlets carry SoffSeal or Metro Rubber products. Both are excellent products, but the two companies have very different philosophies of weatherstrip design. The SoffSeal weatherstrips are square-edged and just a tad oversized compared to GM originals, whereas the Metro Rubber seals are more rounded and closer in size to the originals. You can't go wrong with either brand of seals, but old-car buffs tell me the SoffSeal weatherstrips take a few months to "break in" until doors and trunk can be closed without extra effort.

Installing new weatherstripping is an easy job for the do-it-yourselfer. First, check the new seals against the old ones to make sure they'll fit. Take your time, measuring things out and doing a "dry run" before pushing in the plastic clips or applying weatherstrip adhesive. Go easy with that adhesive! A little goes a long way, and it's not the easiest stuff to clean up. Now let's put that new rubber to good use.

2. Compare your new weatherstripping against the old to make sure it's a good fit. Always do a dry run before getting out the adhesive. Roll down the windows.

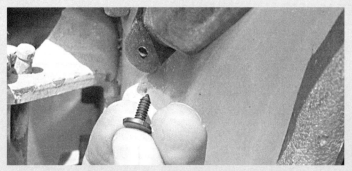

3. Open the door and at the base of the A-pillar you'll find two plastic rivets like this or screws retaining the leading edge of the roof-rail weatherstrip. Remove them and pull the rubber out of its roof channel all the way back to the base of the B-pillar. On 1970–81 Camaros, there will be more rivets or screws at the trailing edge of this weatherstrip as well.

4. Clean out the channel with lacquer thinner and scrape off any residual adhesive or stuck-on rubber. Apply a continuous bead of weatherstrip adhesive to the channel and rear of the roof-rail weatherstrip and push it into the channel, starting at the front. A round-edged putty knife is a help here. Don't use a sharp-edged screwdriver as you might tear the rubber. Use new plastic rivets, if supplied.

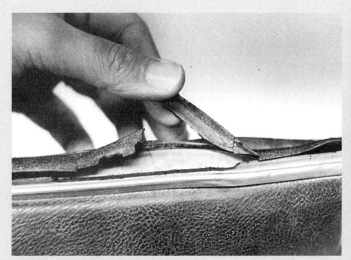

5. Cracked, dried-up window felt can lead to streaks and even scratches on glass.

6. Roll windows down to remove door-window felts and on 1967–69 models, rear-quarter-window felts.

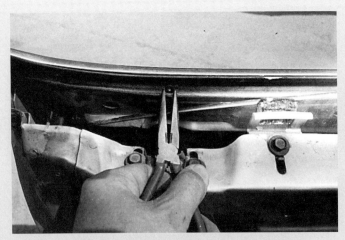

7. It may be necessary to remove interior trim panel and bottom glass stop to gain access to plastic rivets (shown) or short Phillips-head screws on 1970–81 models.

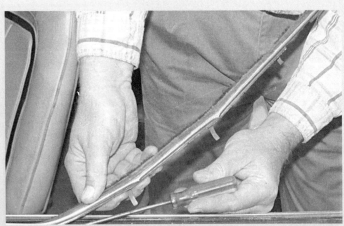

8. On 1967–69 Camaros, outside felts are retained with barbed hooks and screws. After screws at ends are removed, carefully pry up with thin, flat-blade screwdriver and pull the felts free of their barbed hooks.

9. On 1967–69 models, compare the new felts with the old to make sure the location of the hooks lines up. If not, these felts cannot be installed properly without cutting off any hook that doesn't line up and drilling a hole in the felt and sheet metal to install a screw or plastic rivet instead.

10. On 1967–69 models, use your thumbs to firmly press the hooks into their sheet-metal slots in the body.

11. Do the same for the felts at the rear quarter windows of 1967–69 models. If necessary, trim this rubber "wing" to fit into the base of the B-pillar.

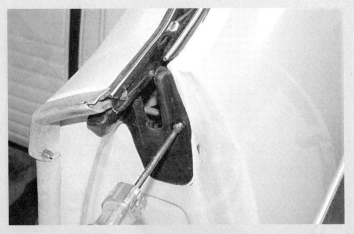

12. Install a new U-shaped seal with rivets or screws for the rear quarter window in the door jamb. A steel "finger" of this seal slips behind the inner felt and is retained with a Phillips-head screw.

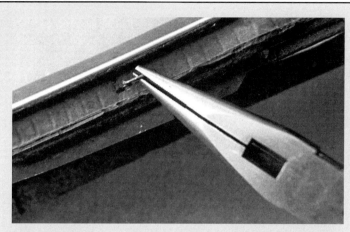

13. Inside door window felts on 1968–81 models are stapled to interior trim panel. To replace, carefully pull out staples. You can reuse the old staples to install new felt by drilling tiny holes for the staple prongs, tapping the staples in, then crimping in place with needle-hose pliers.

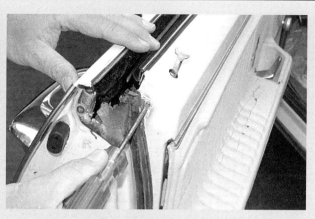

14. Door weatherstripping uses screws or plastic rivets to retain the ends and small plastic "Christmas tree" clips every four inches or so in between. No adhesive is necessary. Some of the end clips may be hidden by paint overspray.

15. New factory-original door weatherstripping comes with new "Christmas tree" clips preinstalled in rubber. Sometimes the old clips stay stuck in the door when the weatherstrip is removed, so pull these out with needle-nose pliers.

16. While the old weatherstripping is removed, it's a good time to clean out any dirt, overspray or corrosion from the door with polishing compound. This will give the door a clean appearance and help prevent future corrosion.

17. Left and right door weatherstrips are not interchangeable. SoffSeal weatherstrips have LEFT or RIGHT molded into their back side.

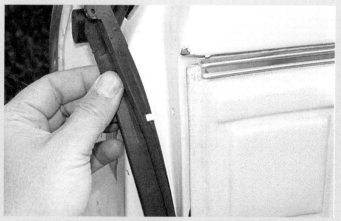

18. Make a "dry run" to be sure you have the correct piece of rubber and it fits correctly, then start by installing the short screws or rivets on one end. If you did your homework, each of the small plastic clips should fit, sometimes with a little coaxing, into a corresponding hole.

19. For stubborn door weatherstrips, a daub or two of weatherstrip adhesive at each end is good insurance.

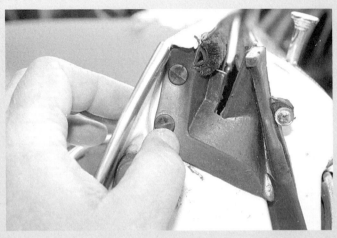

20. Fresh door weatherstrips add a finished appearance to your Camaro.

21. Vertical quarter-window weatherstrip on 1967–69 models should be replaced too. This one slides into a channel from below. Roll the window up for this and use silicone spray to aid installation. If it gets stuck part-way, pull it out and shave tiny amounts of rubber off the new weatherstrip's groove until it slides snugly all the way .

22. On 1967 Camaros, vent-window weatherstrip is the most troublesome of all to install. To replace it, first remove the door trim panel, loosen the side window in its tracks, remove the screws supporting the vent-window post and pull the vent-window assembly up and out of the door. Then disassemble the frame and insert the new triangular-shaped vent-window rubber weatherstrip and a new vertical felt for the side window. This assembly is heavy and real cumbersome. Be extra careful not to damage the glass or scratch the paint on the door.

23. Then reinstall the trim panel and you're done. Not only does replacing the weatherstripping make driving in all kinds of weather more enjoyable, but it is a finishing touch to fresh paint and interior trim on your freshly restored Camaro.

Chapter 15

Door Hinge Repair

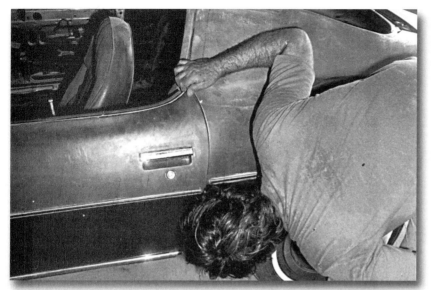

1. Extreme case of door droop. Note large gap at top rear edge of door and misalignment of chrome spears.

If you drive your Camaro on a regular basis, you might be opening and closing the driver's door 20–25 times a day. Multiply that times 365 days a year, and how old did you say your Camaro was?

All 100 pounds or so of each of your Camaro's doors swings on two hinge pins, each about the size of a ball-point pen. The hardened-steel pins ride in sintered-bronze or plastic bushings about the size of a dime. After thousands of openings and closings, the bushings wear out. First the driver's side goes, then the passenger's door. The doors hang lower and lower until you have to physically lift them to latch the striker. Check for the dreaded droopy door syndrome by opening the door, grasping it at the bottom rear and lifting. If you find more than 1/4" of play, the bushings are gonners.

Basically, you've got two options: replace the worn hinges (there are two per door) or rebush the hinges (a kit that does both doors cuts the cost considerably). Either way, you have to remove the doors. By all means, get a helper for this job so you don't drop the door or damage it and the body trying to steady the door on the floor jack.

The lower hinges on 1967–69 models and upper hinges on 1970–81 models incorporate a detent-and-roller assembly. This feature allows your Camaro's door to stay open in one of three positions. If the "ridges" or detents are worn flat, the door will be hard to control in tight parking situations and it's best to replace the entire hinge assembly.

To remove the doors, you'll need a sturdy floor jack to support the door (remember, 100 pounds!), a block of wood to rest the door on and a friend to steady the door during removal and installation. Removing the door trim panel and glass will make it lighter and easier to maneuver, but it's not necessary. Remember to mark with a felt-tip pen or grease pencil the position of the hinges on both the body and door before removing the bolts, so the door can be reinstalled in

Tools & Supplies Needed
- Socket set
- Box-end wrenches
- Felt-tip pen
- Floor jack w/wood block
- Hammer
- Jacksaw
- Drift pin
- Flat-blade screwdrivers
- Bailing wire
- Chisel or rotary grinder
- Vise
- Bushing, pin, and detent roller kit

the same position. If you don't, alignment and adjustment will take much longer.

To rebuild the hinges, you'll need a sturdy workbench and vise. The blacksmithing basically boils down to driving out the old pins and bushings and driving in the new ones. How you remove the old pins depends upon what tools you have available. You can remove the factory "upset" or peened-over area of the old pins with a small die grinder or cut the pins in half with a hacksaw. Drive out the old pieces with a hammer and punch. Depending on what aftermarket supplier manufactured your replacement pins, they are either an interference fit or held in place with circlips.

On the hinge with the detent roller, the spring must be dealt with first before disassembling that hinge pin. Wear eye protection for this, to prevent injury from a flying spring. Insert a stout screwdriver through the center of the spring lengthwise, then carefully pry one end of the spring off its boss on the hinge assembly. After installing a new pin, bushings and detent roller, the spring must be reinstalled.

Compress the spring in a vise and secure it in the compressed position with heavy bailing wire. After levering the compressed spring into position on the hinge assembly, cut the wire and the spring will expand into place. Remove the wire remnants.

When it's time to install the door, first mount the hinges to the body, then the door to the hinges. Behind the body sheet metal is a sliding nut plate that's threaded for the hinge bolts; you may need an awl or ice pick to align the nut plate with the body sheet metal holes.

The door can be adjusted up, down, forward and back where the hinges mount to the body; in and out where the hinges mount to the door. Shoot for a 1/4" gap at the rocker panel, 11/64" at the rear quarter panel and 7/32" at the front fender.

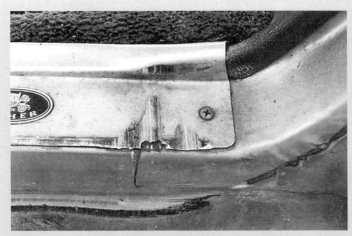

2. Worn sill plate is a dead giveaway of worn hinges, chewed up by scuffing against lower rear edge of door.

3. Replace any worn strikers using a Torx-head socket. This one was hammered into an oblong shape trying to hold the door up.

4. With the door supported on a jack and steadied by a helper, remove the six hinge-to-door bolts first.

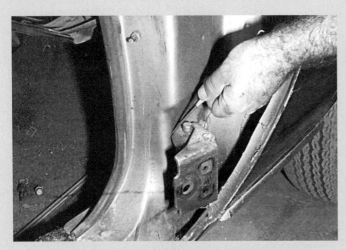

5. Don't forget to trace the outline of the hinges on the door and body to facilitate installation.

6. Start with the hinges that don't have detent springs and rollers. Grind off the upset metal from the tapered (lower) part of the pin, or cut the pin in half with a hacksaw as shown.

7. Invert the hinge and drive out the old pin (or two pin halves) with a hammer and drift.

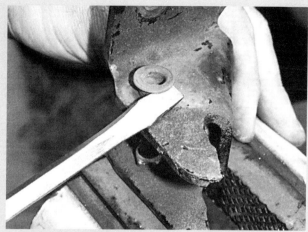

8. Old bushings can usually be levered out with a screwdriver. If stuck, drive them out with another drift.

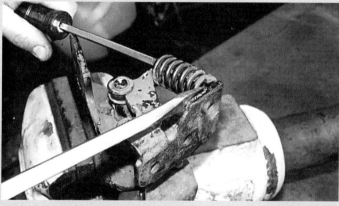

9. Make sure you're wearing eye protection for the next operation. Put the hinge assembly with the detent roller in a vise. Run a long, thin screwdriver through the detent spring as shown on this 1968–69 example, and carefully pry one end of the spring loose with another large flat-blade screwdriver.

10. Once the spring is safely out, cut or drive out the hinge pin and detent roller shaft as you did before.

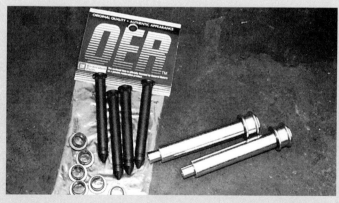

11. Hardened steel pins, sintered bronze bushings and (on 1968–69 models) new detent rollers can make your Camaro's doors hang like new. They can be repaired with this kit from Classic Industries. A different detent-roller kit is available for 1967 models. If detent rollers are worn out on 1970–81 models, entire hinge assembly must be replaced.

12. Carefully tap new bushings into position, shouldered ends facing outboard. Use a light touch. A small body hammer works well here.

13. Note that bushings have different diameters and some, like this one, have serrated edges.

14. Drive in a new detent roller shaft, if removed, as shown on this 1968–69 model.

15. Reassemble the hinge with a new pin. Stake the pin in position just above its tapered end, or use the circlips provided. Apply a light coat of Lubriplate or equivalent to all wear surfaces.

16. To reinstall the detent roller spring, compress it in a vise (wear eye protection!), slip heavy bailing wire through its ends and twist the ends of the wire tight to keep the spring compressed. You've just constructed a mini spring compressor.

17. Then with the wire still holding the spring compressed, lever the spring into the hinge and onto its perches with a screwdriver. Once the spring is securely in place, cut and remove the wire.

18. Mount the hinges to the body and align with the marks you made earlier. To start the first hinge bolts in their holes in the body, it may be necessary to align the sliding nut plates inside the body with an ice pick or Phillips-head screwdriver. Once you get the first bolt started, the other bolt holes should line up easily.

19. Whatever you do, never try to mount a door yourself. If it drops you may hurt yourself and dent the door! Get an assistant to support the door while you make final adjustments and tighten the hinge bolts.

ELECTRICAL

Chapter 16
Servicing RS Headlamps ('67–'69)

1. What sets a 1967–69 Rally Sport apart from other Camaros are its headlamps.

Before the age of aero headlamps, ground-effect skirts and huge spoilers, one of the more popular methods of customizing a basic design was to conceal old sealed-beam headlamps behind movable doors in the grille or fenders. Chevy's opening salvo in the ponycar wars of the late 1960s included such a special Camaro model, the Z22 Rally Sport (RS), its most identifying feature being a set of hideaway headlamps.

Of the 3/4 million or so first-generation Camaros produced from 1967 through 1969, only about 140,000 are RSs. And you could combine the hideaway headlamps of the RS (Z22) with the SS or Z28 option, but the SS or Z28 remained the dominant trim group. Whereas the limited production and novelty of the 1967–69 RS cars aids desirability and value, the complexity of the hideaway-headlamp system can be a real pain in the wallet if it's not working properly. Two systems were used: 1967 models feature a system with electric motors to open and close the doors covering the headlamps, while 1968–69 RSs utilize a vacuum system.

The 1967 system works thusly: Power is taken from the horn relay junction block, through a 10-amp circuit breaker and three relays located on a removable panel in the engine compartment under the left front fender, to an electric motor and a pair of start/stop limit switches at each headlamp door. The doors open when the dash-mounted headlamp switch is pulled out to the "on" position; they close only when the headlamp switch is turned off when the ignition is in the "on" or "acc" position.

The most common problem on 1967 RS models is chewed up gears on the electric motors. Original-equipment motors used plastic gears that stripped out easily if the doors were forced open or closed by hand. Aftermarket motors with steel gears are now available. Motors could also burn out if binding in the linkage caused a door to stick part way open

or closed, or if the limit switches were improperly adjusted, causing the motors to run constantly until they overheated and failed. You'll need a voltmeter, continuity tester and a wiring diagram to check out a malfunctioning RS headlamp circuit.

With the vacuum-operated system on 1968–69 models, vacuum leaks—or more technically correct, air leaks—occurring almost anywhere in the yards of vacuum hose, plus numerous tees and canisters are often the culprits. The system routes manifold vacuum, via the dash-mounted headlamp switch, to an engine-compartment-mounted vacuum reservoir and relay, which in turn directs the vacuum to an actuator canister below each headlamp door. Inside each actuator is a large diaphragm which acts on a rod attached to each headlamp-door bellcrank.

Even when airtight, sub-freezing weather can cause the doors to stick closed. This is why Chevrolet redesigned the headlamp doors for 1969 with see-through panes so the headlamps could shine through closed doors in the event of a malfunction. When working the kinks out of a 1968–69 RS headlamp system, your primary troubleshooting weapon is a simple vacuum pump. Start at the manifold source and slowly, methodically work your way down to each actuator.

Add up the numerous brackets, levers, pivot bolts, special washers, bellcranks and so forth and it would suffice to say that there's a lot going on behind that grille. Aside from the tangle of wires, circuit breakers, limit switches and relays on 1967 models, and yards of vacuum hose, check valves, tee-fittings and actuators on 1968–69 models, the mechanical linkage for each headlamp door assembly must be free of corrosion, binding, misalignment or collision damage that would prevent free movement.

Here are some tips to keep your 1967–69 RS hideaway headlamps working in tip-top shape.

2. When the lights are switched off, automatic headlamp covers hide the lamps and give a custom grille appearance.

3. Trouble is, sometimes the doors don't operate properly. Here, scratch marks show these headlamp doors are binding against surrounding trim. Either move the trim or adjust the door covers to eliminate the interference.

4. To adjust position of headlamp covers on doors, loosen four Phillips-head screws, slide cover up or down on door backing plate, and retighten. Aim for a gap of 0.04–0.170" between door and grille bezel.

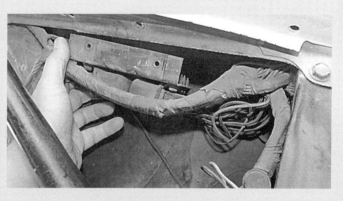

5. A bank of three relays and a circuit breaker live under left fender of '67 RS. Pull windshield-washer bottle, remove two hex screws and tilt down panel, to inspect relays and circuit breaker for headlamp doors.

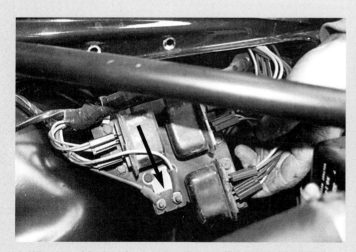

6. When troubleshooting, relays should click when headlamps are switched on and off. Most common gremlin here is a faulty 10-amp circuit breaker (arrow).

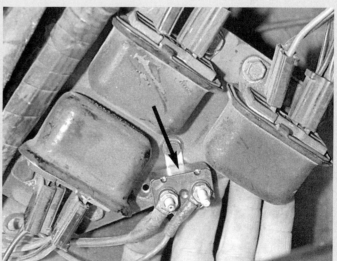

7. Original Delco Remy replacement is no longer available, but this Standard BR8 10-amp relay (arrow) from an early 1970s Dodge works perfectly with minor bracket modifications.

8. Doorbell buzzer lookalike (arrow) is actually one of two limit switches for each front headlamp on '67 RS models. One opens circuit to electric motor when headlamp door is fully closed and another one does same when door is fully open. If headlamp door gets stuck midway, electric motor will run indefinitely until it fries or battery is discharged—unless you disconnect battery.

9. To work on passenger-side headlamp, disconnect and remove battery. Unbolt and remove battery tray. One of two headlamp-housing-to-radiator-support bolts is hidden under battery tray. The other two headlamp housing bolts go into the fender and are directly accessible from the front after opening the headlamp doors and removing its bezel.

10. Remove small nut at bottom of headlamp hinge, then pull out long headlamp hinge bolt.

11. Then remove short hex screw retaining headlamp door to motor arm and lift out hinge and headlamp door as an assembly. Sealed beam was removed for more wrench-swinging room, but it can stay on headlamp housing, if desired.

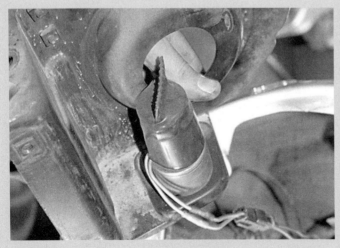

12. Pull out headlamp housing and disconnect motor lead at junction.

13. When replacing headlamp motor, first mark position of crank arm for assembly reference. Remove nut from motor shaft and lift off crank arm, noting number and placement of steel and fiber washers. On assembly, use light coating of Lubriplate between washers. Don't overtighten shaft nut; just make sure it is snug.

14. Aftermarket '67 RS headlamp motor and mounting bracket assembly bolts in place of original unit and is functionally identical, except for using more durable steel drive gears instead of GM's fragile plastic ones.

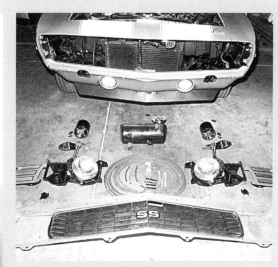

15. Vacuum-operated system on the 1968–69 Rally Sports has more than a few moving parts. Shown is the 1969 system.

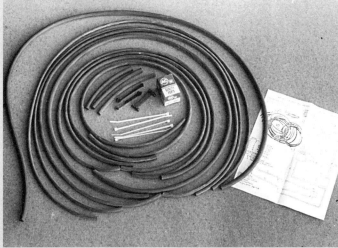

16. Chasing air leaks underhood on yard after yard of dried, cracked old vacuum hose can be frustrating and time-consuming. Better to start from scratch with this color-coded hose kit with instructions such as this one from Classic Industries.

17. When installing new hoses, start at a reliable source of manifold vacuum and work forward. Install filter (arrow) near vacuum source then install tee. One hose goes to dash-mounted headlamp switch; another goes to relay on vacuum reservoir.

18. Conventional Camaro headlamp switch at left doesn't have vacuum ports unique to 1968–69 RS switch at right.

19. Vacuum relay on 1968–69 RS has numerous hoses sprouting from it. Carefully follow routing diagram in hose kit.

20. Mounted under forward edge of front wheel well of '68–'69 RS models is this soup-can-sized canister, called a vacuum actuator. Because of its location, it's subject to road damage and corrosion. Two vacuum hoses attach to it, one to open the door and the other to close it. Test the actuator bellows with a vacuum pump.

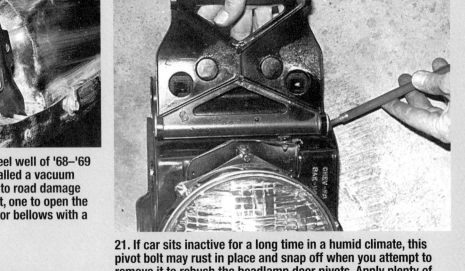

21. If car sits inactive for a long time in a humid climate, this pivot bolt may rust in place and snap off when you attempt to remove it to rebush the headlamp door pivots. Apply plenty of penetrating oil and don't use excessive force.

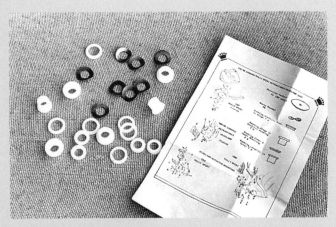

22. As you can see from this kit, not just any bushing, washer or grommet will do. Instruction sheet details where each piece goes for correct system operation.

23. One of many locations that requires specially stepped bushings are these headlamp door pivots.

24. After the system is back together, check headlamp-door operation before venturing out at night.

Chapter 17

Replacing the Front Wiring

1. It may look like a rope trick gone bad, but if you go slow and take each wire one at a time, installing a new harness is easy. Here, Larry Wright sorts out a front lighting harness for installation in a '73 Rally Sport.

After of decades of exposure to the elements, not to mention road salt, engine heat, oil, battery acid, gasoline or perhaps a ham-fisted previous owner, your vintage Camaro's wiring may be in need of replacement. Maybe the culprit is a corroded connector that refuses to let one more electron pass through. Perhaps it's a pack rat or squirrel that's decided to redecorate the inside of his nest with chunks of your Camaro's wires. Or possibly some insulation has chafed through, exposing bare wire and short-circuiting to ground. And don't discount the possibility that the poor splices and dried up electrical tape of some previous body repair or aftermarket electrical accessory such as fog lights, a towing harness, theft alarm or sound system have finally gone bad.

Basically, most wiring forward of the firewall is grouped into two main harnesses: the front lighting circuit and the engine circuit. On the 1973 Rally Sport, for example, the front lighting harness services the headlamps, front parking/turn-signal lamps, side markers, horn and horn relay, brake pressure-differential warning lamp, wiper motor and washer pump. The engine harness acts as central nervous system for the ignition coil, starter solenoid, oil-pressure warning lamp, temperature sending unit, alternator, voltage regulator and vacuum-advance solenoid. Options such as full instrumentation and accessories like air conditioning will add their own circuits. Year-to-year variations exist, however, so check the Chevrolet service manual for the year Camaro you are working on.

If you have an obviously faulty wire or connector, it can be replaced individually. Be sure to match the wire gauge (Camaros use 12, 14, 16, 18 or 20-gauge wire under the hood) so the new wire can handle the amount of current that circuit was designed to carry. Better yet, find a donor car of the same model year and equipment and snag as much good wire and connectors from the harness as possible. Match the color codes. Most connectors use spade terminals that can be

Tools & Supplies Needed
- Small socket set
- Small open-end wrench set
- Small box-end wrench set
- Flat-blade screwdriver
- Dielectric grease
- Replacement side-marker bulbs (194)
- Replacement wiring harness

carefully disassembled using a small flat-blade screwdriver and needle-nose pliers.

A word to the wise, though. If a section of your Camaro's wiring got absolutely fried, or if a fuse blows repeatedly, better troubleshoot the cause of the electrical malady before laying in new wire. Also, make sure each component is grounded properly and that corrosion isn't inhibiting a good metal-to-metal contact. Check that the braided ground strap/s connecting the rear of the cylinder head/s to the firewall are not broken or disconnected.

Avoid splicing in new sections of wire if at all possible. The splice then becomes the weak point in the circuit; electrical tape may dry out and fall off, exposing bare wire to short circuits or corrosion. If you absolutely have to splice some wire, crimp the loose ends into male and female spade connectors, solder in place and cover the joint with shrink-wrap insulation for a weatherproof seal.

The best way to undertake a restoration, though, is to replace a damaged harness with a new one. High-quality reproduction harnesses are available from a variety of mail-order houses. This is money well spent, as these harnesses contain all of the correct-gauge, color-coded wires precut to factory length, the right snap-fit connectors, sheathing and cable ties. All you have to do is go slow and mark each wire with a flag identifying which components it connects to.

Once the old harness is removed, lay it down next to your replacement harness to make sure you have the correct part. And if you plan on replacing more than one harness, do them one at a time to avoid a tangle of confusion.

Be smart about where you route wires. Stay away from hot exhaust manifolds and sharp edges that cut or abrade the insulation. Use the firewall-mounted plastic gutter and the front fender harness ties to guide and keep the wires organized in bunches. Whenever a wire passes through a bulkhead, use a rubber grommet to protect the insulation. If possible, follow the applicable wiring diagram in a Chevrolet factory service manual or reproduction literature.

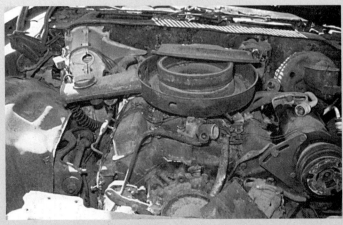

2. An engine fire destroyed the wiring in this '79 Camaro. Usually, you're not dealing with damage this severe, but a complete harness with color-coded, pre-cut wires and factory connectors takes away the guesswork.

3. Or perhaps you're returning a customized Camaro to stock condition as with this '78 pro-street Z28. Once the custom engine pieces are removed, you'll be way ahead by installing a new engine and front-lighting harness.

4. Disconnect the battery cables. And because you'll need to get in front of the battery to work on the lighting harness, remove the fender-to-radiator-support brace on that side and lift out the battery.

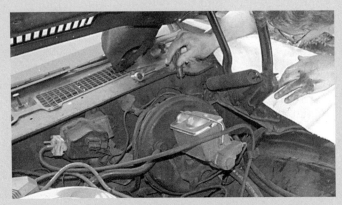

5. The front-lighting and engine harnesses connect to the main junction at the firewall. On 1970-and-later Camaros with power brakes, the junction is buried down behind the brake booster. To disconnect harness connector, use a 3/8" socket to remove the connector hex screw and pry the harness connector from the firewall with a long, flat-blade screwdriver.

6. Front-lighting harness from 1970 and later models incorporates wire leads for wiper motor and washer, horn(s) and horn relay, brake warning light, plus headlamps, front park/turn-signal lamps and side-marker lamps. Using a flat-blade screwdriver, lever front-wiring harness terminal out of junction.

7. One by one, disconnect terminals from old harness and plug in terminals from new harness. Do this slowly, methodically, and everything should match up. At firewall, start by connecting two-prong female spades to front and bottom of wiper motor, and single-prong spade to washer pump.

8. At horn relay on firewall, connect two single spade terminals. Don't forget to route wires as they were originally installed, such as behind and under brake booster.

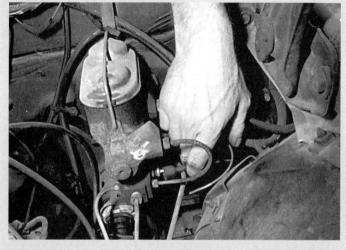

9. Shown here on a '67 Camaro, connect female bullet connector to brake master cylinder warning light switch.

10. Move the evaporative canister out of the way to get to driver's side connectors for headlight and side marker.

11. Remove two hex screws for radiator shroud.

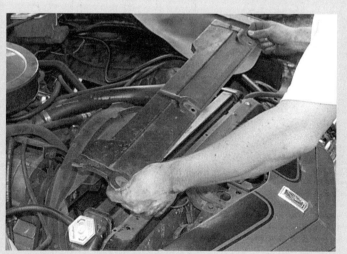

12. Remove three hex screws for radiator-support cover and lift off cover to gain access to harness.

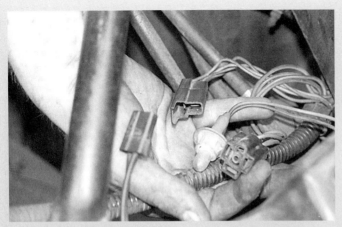

13. Disconnect leads for park/turn-signal lamps, headlamps and side markers from old harness and plug them into new one.

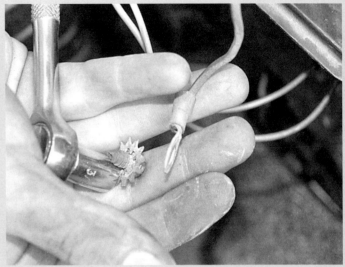

14. Good grounds are essential to complete any circuit. Ground wire at radiator support should have star washer underneath ring terminal for proper metal-to-metal contact.

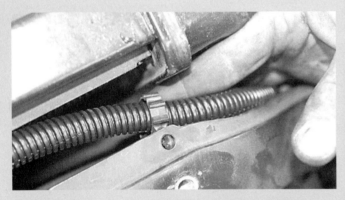

15. Front-lighting harness is routed in front of radiator just beneath upper lip of radiator support. These plastic clips keep it from sagging down in front of radiator cooling fins and out of harm's way.

16. Connect lead for horn(s) through holes in radiator support.

17. On 1968 and later cars, front-lighting harness ends at side-marker lamps, one of which has been removed for clarity. Twist socket 90 degrees to remove from side-marker assembly. Use new 194 bulb if available.

18. Daub some dielectric grease on the harness main connector for a water-tight connection.

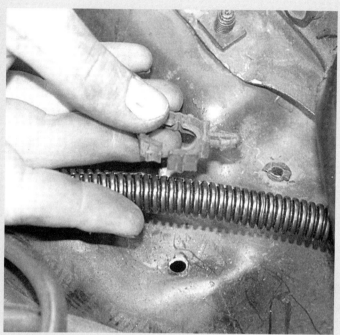

19. Use clips provided with harness and holes in fender liner to neatly route harness along left side of engine compartment.

20. Reconnect harness to firewall junction and install retaining screw. Now connect the battery and test the operation of the lights, wipers and horn. Your Camaro's underhood electrics should be on their way to operating in tip-top condition.

Chapter 18

Horn Troubleshooting

1. Pry off the center cap, remove the three Phillips-head screws and lift out the plastic ring.

It's surprising how many older Camaros are running around without benefit of a working horn. This is more than just another restoration item; it's a safety issue. In almost every case, the horn or horns is/are in perfect working order. It's the wiring or the relay that's at fault.

Sometimes the problem might be caused by a bad ground due to corrosion or an over-exuberant painter. Quite often, the malfunction may be caused by incorrect assembly of the small parts under the horn button on the steering wheel by a do-it-yourselfer.

Here's how you do it on a 1967–68 Camaro with a deluxe wheel.

2. Lift out the center cap retainer.

3. Then lift out the large spring washer and plastic ring. If any of these parts are missing or installed differently from shown here, the horn button may not have been grounded properly.

4. Hook up a 12-volt continuity tester between the black ground wire at the horn relay and the spring-loaded button on the steering wheel hub. If the lightbulb lights, the wire between the horn button and relay is good. Make sure the spring-loaded button is free to move.

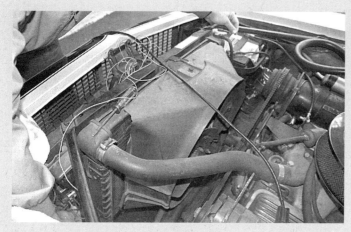

5. Install a jumper wire from the positive terminal of the battery to the dark green wire at the relay. If the horns beep, they are not the problem.

6. Check for power to the relay. Install a voltmeter between the negative battery terminal and the red relay wire. If it reads at or close to 12 volts, the relay is getting juice.

7. It never hurts to check the horn connectors for corrosion or a loose fit, either.

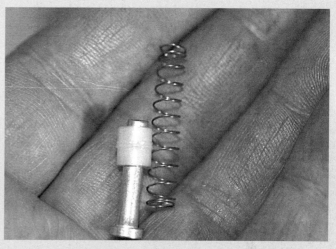

8. If this small plunger is missing or isn't spring-loaded, remove the steering wheel (see steering wheel section, page 15) and inspect. Check to make sure spring isn't damaged.

9. With these checks, you should be able to isolate any problems in the circuit. Be sure to install the horn button components exactly as they were removed and your Camaro will have the pipes to sound off loud and clear when it has to.

Chapter 19
Radio Upgrade

1. Sometimes the original is not the greatest. Our '67 Camaro's original Delco AM monaural radio was tired and feeble by today's audio standards. But to give the old squawk box the heave-ho, we first had to remove a lot of underdash items starting with the glove box door. Disconnect the battery.

No matter how much you love your '60s or '70s Camaro, there are a lot of things today's models do better. Back in the '60s, most cars came with AM radios only. Have you listened to AM radio lately? Sure, there's news, weather, traffic and sports and talk show callers who need to get a life. But all the good music switched to FM decades ago. Or maybe your Camaro has an early Delco AM/FM, with poor signal strength and saddled with a scratchy 6x9"oval speaker with a dinky magnet; two ovals if your car had the optional rear deck speaker. Not exactly the Big Sound you had in mind for cruising the strip.

Not to mention cassette tapes for just the right music to set that all-important mood. Or if you're really into the best music-reproduction fidelity money can buy, a compact disc player. Oh, and some decent speakers to cover life's crystal-smashing highs, rumbling lows and soul-searching mid-range.

But no one with an ounce of sense wants to butcher the dash or cut speaker holes in the doors, kick panels, rear quarter trim panels or rear deck of a vintage Camaro. Not me, anyway, even though I like to drive my 1967 RS occasionally and won't treat it like some museum piece. Sure, if yours is a show car with everything original right down to date-coded hose clamps, an aftermarket sound system in place of that static old Delco is pure anathema. Another possibility would be to pop for one of those "stealth" sound systems. These have the guts of a modern Japanese radio stuffed into the shell of the trusty Delco. Only your bank account will know for sure as these babies are expensive.

Enter Custom Autosound of Anaheim, California. Custom Autosound is in the business of selling new car audio equipment for older cars. It's possible to install today's music hall surround sound in yesterday's package without resorting to any blacksmithing.

Custom Autosound manufactures several lines of shaft-mounted replacement radios and cassette players that install in the original dash openings. Additionally, Custom

Tools & Supplies Needed
- New head unit and speakers
- Needle-nose pliers
- Wire crimper/cutter
- Phillips-head screwdriver
- Set of small-size, deep-well hex sockets
- Drop light
- Blanket or two to lay across the seat and sill to pad your back a bit

Autosound sells a full complement of Pioneer and Kenwood head units, plus wide-response speakers, amplifiers, alarm systems, trunk-mounted CD changers and much more for 1967–77 Camaros. Super trick offerings include "stealth" subwoofers from Pioneer; a briefcase-size unit that attaches to the rear seatback and a hubcap-size unit that actually fits inside the spare tire wheel. Utilizing tandem-duct reflex technology, these generate high-quality bass without the drone commonly associated with "boom boxes." And they're out of sight so no one need know. Ditto for Velcro-mounted underseat "cabinet sound" speakers.

Depending on the year and options on your Camaro, installing a new sound system ranges from a relaxed one-hour job to an intense all-day marathon. If your Camaro has air conditioning as our '67 RS does, fishing out the original underdash speaker and installing new ones in the original location requires patience. But once everything's buttoned up and you switch on the new system for the first time, you'll realize why a few years back Chevy dubbed the Camaro "the official car of rock and roll."

Note: Since the first edition, technology has obviously changed quite a bit, but the install procedures are bascially the same.

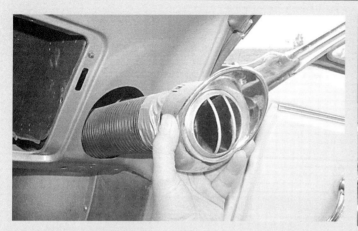

2. Remove the two Phillips-head screws for the right ventilation duct (if so equipped) and pull out the duct and its flex hose. This gives some room to remove the glove box liner.

3. Slide the ashtray out and remove it. Then remove the four Phillips-head screws retaining the bottom edge of the dash center trim panel.

4. Pull off the old radio knobs and adjusters and remove the two shaft nuts using a deep-well socket. Then lift off the radio trim plate and the center trim panel.

5. If equipped with air conditioning, remove the two Phillips-head screws for the center A/C outlet.

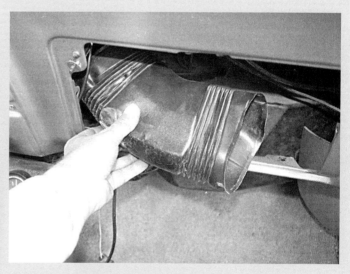

6. Remove the two Phillips-head screws retaining the radio to the dash, then the four hex screws for the ventilation controls above it.

7. On air-conditioned cars, pull out this flexible plastic duct...

8. ...then this center A/C register.

9. Remove the hex screw for the factory front speaker brace.

10. Disconnect the factory speaker wire. Wiggle the front speaker out through the upper part of the center duct opening, above the ventilation controls.

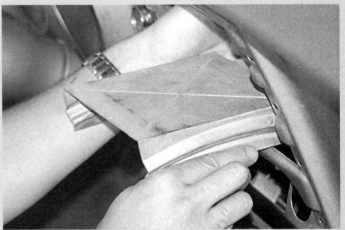

11. Remove the screws for the ashtray slider mechanism and remove the slider.

12. Disconnect the radio antenna and power lead. Lift the ventilation controls up, turn the old radio sideways and slide it out through the center duct opening under the ventilation controls.

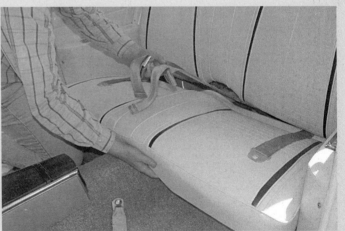

13. To route the rear speaker wires back to the rear package shelf, it's necessary to remove the rear seats and left rear quarter trim panel. Start with the rear seat cushion, pushing it rearward as you lift up to disengage it from hooks in the floor.

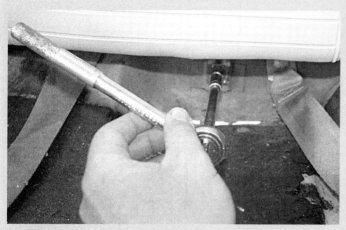

14. Next, remove the two hex screws at the bottom of the rear seatback and lift out the seatback.

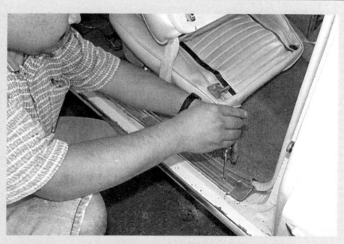

15. Remove the four Phillips-head screws and lift off the driver's side sill plate.

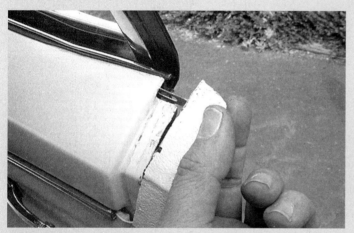

16. After removing one Phillips-head screw hidden in the front of the rear quarter window weatherstrip channel, pull off the windlace

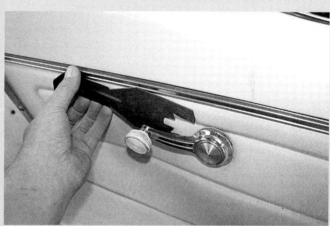

17. Remove the rear window winder using the special horseshoe-clip removal tool.

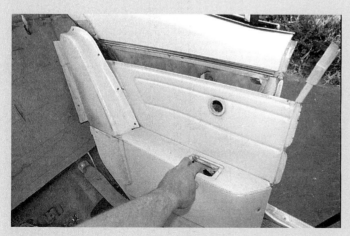

18. After removing the Phillips-head screws at the front and rear of the driver's side rear quarter trim panel, lift it out.

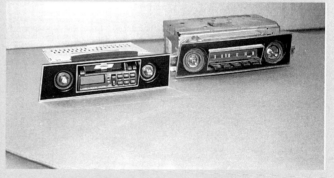

19. Custom Autosound's top choice is this Kenwood KNW-800 AM/FM radio/cassette/CD controller, with 18 station presets, Dolby noise reduction, metal tape capability and a whopping 60 watts of power. Despite its many features, Kenwood KNW-800 is noticeably smaller and lighter than old Delco AM unit at right. Don't forget to match shaft length with old radio by adjusting position of nuts on shafts of new radio.

20. At the rear, we installed a pair of Autosound's best midrange twin-cone 6x9"speakers. For stealth appearance, we mounted them under the rear package shelf with no exposed grilles. Measure distance from radio to rear speaker, then add some more. Better to have more wire than you need rather than splice together short sections. Use high-quality automotive speaker wire. Hook up wire leads to rear speakers and route them along base of left rear quarter trim panel.

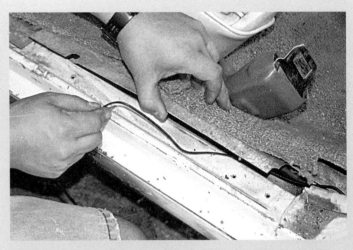

21. Remove the sheet-metal screws for the sill channel on the driver's side and lay the rear speaker wires inside.

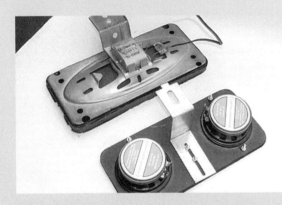

22. For the front, dual Custom Autosound 4" tweeters with large cobalt ferrite magnets give 30 watts each of stereo sound, yet bolt right up in factory-original location of single speaker. Custom bracketry for underdash speakers makes installation a snap. Tip: Paint speaker panel screw heads flat black so they're not visible through windshield.

23. Trial-fit front speaker in dash then adjust bracket nuts to suit.

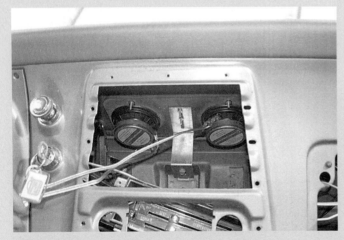

24. Snug as a bug, Custom Autosound speakers mount with bracket against firewall. Hook up speaker lead wires.

25. Fish rear speaker wires under left kick panel and up over steering column. Cable-tie wires to underdash so they don't hang down around your feet.

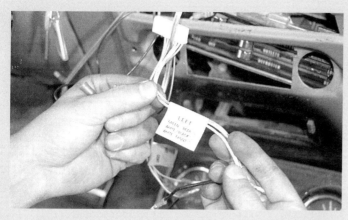

26. Here's where, hopefully, Stanley meets Livingston, so to speak. Identifier flags in kit take guesswork out of which wires connect to what.

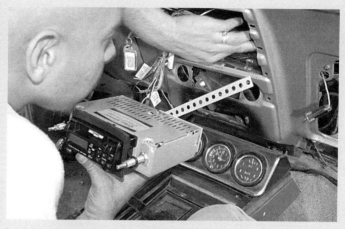

27. Attach a flexible rear support strap onto the back of the radio and find a good spot to mount it to.

28. Slide the radio through the dash opening under the ventilation controls, supporting underneath it through the ashtray opening. Connect the antenna.

29. Install these large rectangular spring washers on the radio shafts behind the dash.

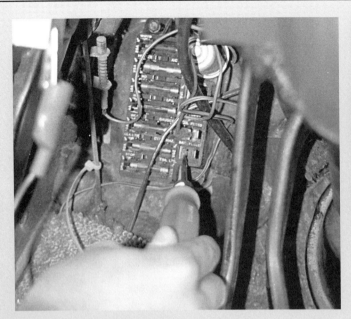

30. At the fuse box, find a good 12-volt power source and plug in the new radio's power lead.

31. Install the rear seat, left rear quarter trim panel, sill plate and all of the underdash items removed earlier to gain access to the radio and front speaker. When installing radio tuning adjusters under knobs, left "wing" goes on at 8 o'clock and right wing installs at 4 o'clock. Line up ears on adjusters with slots on shafts.

32. With custom auto sounds in our Camaro courtesy of the experts at Custom Autosound, there are no ugly door or rear deck speakers shouting aftermarket.

ENGINE
&
DRIVETRAIN

Chapter 20
Distributor Overhaul

1. After decades of service, the breaker-point distributor in your 1967–74 Camaro deserves a thorough going-through to assure top-notch operation. To remove the distributor on a Chevy V-8, first depress and rotate 90 degrees the two hold-down clamps, lift off the distributor cap and crank the engine over so the rotor is pointing to the number one cylinder spark-plug wire and the engine is at top dead center, as shown. Mark the position of the rotor on the distributor body with grease pencil. Then remove the distributor hold-down bracket and bolt and pull the distributor straight up. The rotor will turn as the distributor is removed because its drive gear is helical.

The breaker-point type distributor used on most 1967–74 Camaros will give years of dependable service provided the points are kept in adjustment and the points, condenser, cap and rotor are replaced periodically, say every 12,000–15,000 miles. But after decades and perhaps several hundred thousands of miles of use, the distributor should get a thorough going through.

Sitting in the engine compartment, the distributor is subjected to engine heat, road grit, oil, moisture and road salt. Previous ham-fisted mechanics may have chewed up the screws for the points, condenser and breaker plate, making them difficult to tighten securely. You'll want to ascertain that the centrifugal and vacuum advance mechanisms are working properly. Also, check for frayed wires, especially the coil lead and rubber grommet that route through the distributor body.

Overall, your Camaro's distributor might just be in need of a good cleaning and lubrication, and doing that can give you piece of mind. You'll want to remove any buildup of grease or oil that might interfere with the function of the breaker points. Also, now's the time to remove any corrosion buildup with a small wire brush.

Once the distributor is apart, important wear points to check include the breaker cam lobes, distributor shaft (and bushings) and the drive gear. If the rubbing block of the points wore down to its hard backing or if the points were run without cam lube, the lobes of the distributor shaft cam could be worn to the extent the points no longer open and close to specification; that affects dwell and dwell affects timing. If this is the case, replace the breaker cam assembly with one from another distributor. The part is not serviced separately.

Tools & Supplies Needed
- Slot-head screwdriver
- Hammer
- Drift pin or punch (11/64")
- Wood blocks (1x2x4")
- Vacuum pump
- Carb cleaner, solvent or brake cleaner
- Non-oxidizing grease
- Moly assembly lube
- Motor oil
- Breaker point cam lube
- Crocus cloth
- Ignition point file
- Chalk or grease pencil

Parts Needed
- Breaker points
- Condenser
- Rotor
- Distributor cap
- Vacuum canister (optional)
- Centrifugal advance weights and springs (optional)
- Breaker plate screws (optional)
- Felt washer (optional)
- Felt washer retainer (optional)
- Coil lead wire and grommet (optional)

The shaft should spin freely in the distributor body with virtually no side play. End play should be in the 0.02-0.09" range. It's controlled by a 0.03" thick shim between the drive gear and distributor body. The GM part number for this shim is 1927529, but it's no longer available from Chevrolet. Instead, try an aftermarket source such as Year One.

Also, visually check the distributor shaft for scoring, both where it rides in its bushings and at the bottom where it indexes into the oil-pump drive. Dress minor scratches that catch a fingernail with crocus cloth. A shaft with deep scoring should be replaced and the two oilite bushings pressed out and new ones installed. Bushing replacement is a major repair and unless the distributor in question is a rare part number, it's much more cost-effective to find another good used unit. Replacement bushings are available (along with a bushing installation driver) from some of the Corvette parts outlets such as Corvette Central and Chicago Corvette.

Those oilite bushings are lubricated by non-oxidizing grease in a well in the distributor body. After decades of use, the grease dries up. When you rebuild the distributor, clean out the well, fill it about two-thirds full of grease and install a new plastic retainer. The retainer and washer-shaped felt wick for the breaker plate are also available from Chicago Corvette and Corvette Central.

If the cast-iron distributor drive gear is worn, it can be replaced separately. It's available from Camaro parts sources such as Classic Industries. Remember, the distributor drive gear is driven by the camshaft, so if you switch to a steel billet cam, use a bronze gear on the distributor.

The reason Delco made scores of distributors for Camaros in any given year was to tune them for specific applications: i.e. engine displacement, transmission, emission controls, body style, A/C or non A/C and so on. If you get a used distributor from a junkyard, you have only a slim chance of finding one that is calibrated to work with your car. A lot of the tuning, however,

occurs in the advance mechanisms. Since these are wear items, you can turn a problem into an opportunity by replacing the vacuum advance canister and centrifugal advance springs with ones that are calibrated for your application. NOS GM canisters and an advance-curve tuning kit (with several different sets of springs) are available for many Camaros from Year One.

On an otherwise functional distributor, check the vacuum advance with a vacuum pump. If the advance diaphragm is good, it should hold 20" and not leak down. Because the vacuum advance mechanism advances ignition timing only when the engine is cruising under light load, a malfunctioning vacuum canister will result in poor fuel mileage. The centrifugal advance works by spinning a pair of weights against spring pressure; the stiffer the springs, the slower the advance curve and the lighter the springs, the quicker the curve. An old hotrod trick to get more ignition advance quickly was to remove one of the two springs. But on some engines, too much advance too soon, can lead to destructive detonation. And an engine that's pinging under initial part-throttle accelaration may indicate that it needs stiffer advance springs.

You can, of course, update to an electronic breakerless distributor, either one of the fine aftermarket replacement units available or GM's own High Energy Ignition (HEI) setup originally used on all 1975-and-later Camaros. These generally provide a hotter spark, consistent dwell and timing and, of course, don't require periodic point adjustment and replacement. But if originality counts, or if you just like the simplicity and ease of repair of a Delco breaker-point distributor, the stock 1967–74 system is the way to go.

Before you yank out your Camaro's distributor, make things easier by cranking the engine until the number one cylinder is at top dead center and the rotor is pointing to the number-one sparkplug wire position on the distributor. Try not to disturb the engine while the distributor is removed and installation should be a breeze.

2. Remove the rotor, breaker points and condenser.

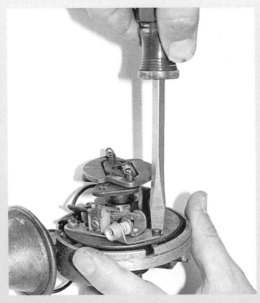

3. Pull off the centrifugal advance springs.

5. Support the gear end of the distributor on a wood block and tap out the drive gear using a hammer and drift.

4. And lift off the centrifugal advance weights.

6. Slide off the drive gear, taking note of the position of the flat washer and tanged washer between it and the distributor housing.

7. Slide out the mainshaft.

8. Lever off this retaining ring and lift the breaker plate off the distributor housing. It will still be connected to the housing via a primary wire lead at this point.

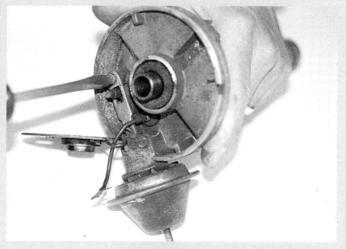

9. Remove the two screws and lift off the vacuum advance unit.

10. From the center of the distributor housing, lever out the felt wick and under it, this plastic retainer.

11. Dried-up grease under retainer needs to be cleaned out.

12. With a small screwdriver, push the rubber grommet for the primary lead wire through the housing and snake out the wire. Often, this wire is cracked and frayed and should be replaced.

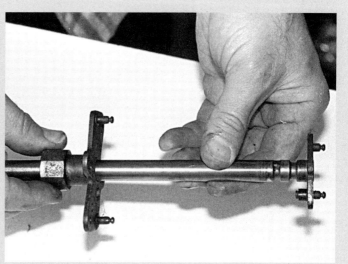

13. Finally, slide the breaker cam off the mainshaft.

14. Give all parts a good scrubbing with solvent.

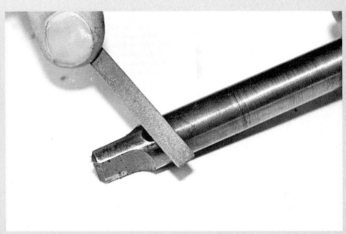

15. Inspect the mainshaft for scoring and serious wear where it slots into the oil pump. We removed small burrs where the drive gear retaining pin inserts.

16. The breaker cam must not show appreciable wear or the points won't open and close to specifications. Replace the breaker cam if worn from lack of lubrication.

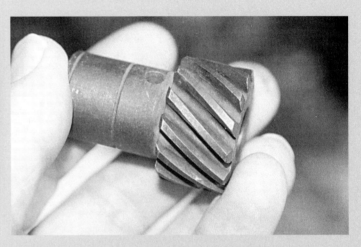

17. Likewise the drive gear should be free of burrs or uneven, excessive wear. Replace the gear if in doubt.

18. Cleaned and inspected, the distributor is ready to go back together.

19. Pack this cavity about half full of non-oxidizing grease.

20. Insert the plastic retainer over the cavity to keep the grease from wicking up onto the breaker plate later on.

21. Install a new felt wick on top of the plastic retainer and apply a few drops of oil.

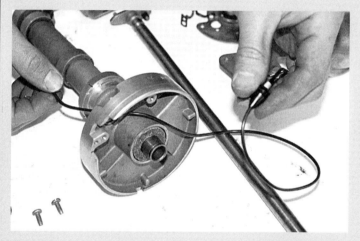

22. Insert the primary wire lead and grommet into the distributor housing.

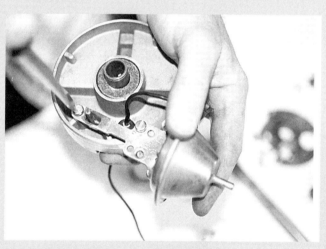

23. Install the vacuum advance mechanism.

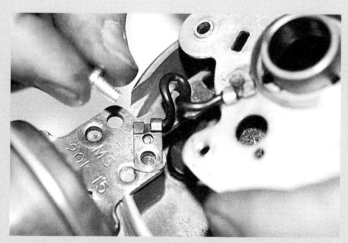

24. Next is the breaker plate. Don't forget to insert this ground wire ring connector on top of the advance unit and UNDER the breaker plate to be captured by one of the advance-unit screws.

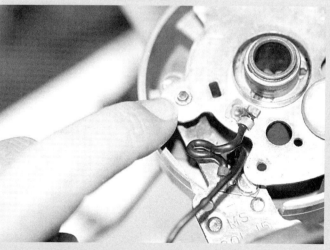

25. Also be sure to hook the advance-unit rod through the hold in the breaker plate.

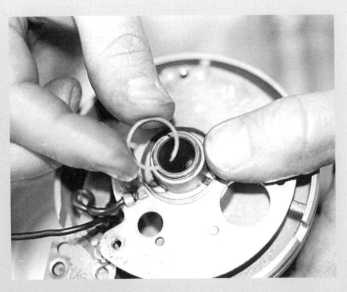

26. Fit a new retaining ring to secure the breaker plate to the distributor housing.

27. Smear some moly grease on the distributor shaft.

28. Install the tanged washer and shim on the shaft, exactly like this.

29. To figure out which way to install the drive gear, temporarily install the rotor and position the drive gear so its dimple or dot aligns with the rotor (arrow).

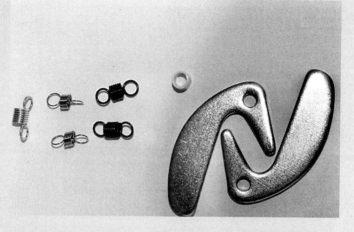

30. Support the drive gear on wood blocks again to install the gear. To keep things aligned, try inserting a small bolt through the opposite end of the gear that will be driven out as you tap in the roll pin.

31. Install the centrifugal weights and springs. This kit from Year One Inc. includes new weights to replace ones with worn-out pin holes and a spring selection. The heavier springs give later centrifugal advance and lighter ones give earlier advance. You can mix and match different ones until you get the right curve for your Camaro, or just stick with the stock GM springs. The kit also includes a new bushing to be used on some distributors on pins under the weight mount.

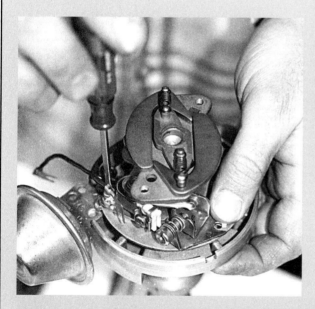

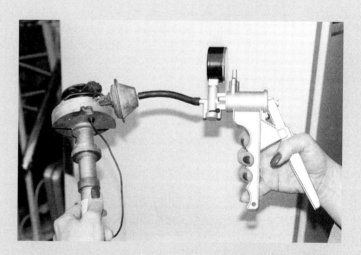

32. Don't forget to install new breaker points and a condenser. Lightly lube the breaker cam with the grease supplied with the points to minimize rubbing block wear.

33. Check the operation of the vacuum-advance unit with a vacuum pump. Depending on your unit's calibration, the rod should start rotating the breaker plate at 7–10" of mercury and have reached full rotation by 15–20". If the rod doesn't move at all, the diaphragm in the advance unit may be leaking, requiring replacement of the advance unit.

Chapter 21
Rochester Quadrajet Overhaul

1. Performance buffs often think a big Holley is what they need, but actually a properly set-up Rochester Quadrajet is a first-class 2-stage fuel metering device.

If you think you need to bolt on the biggest Holley 4150 double-pumper money can buy to make your Camaro a real performance machine, think again. Think Rochester Quadrajet.

The Quadrajet's been installed as original equipment on millions of 1967–85 Camaros, plus many millions of other GM applications. Except for 1967–72 Z28s and some big-block cars, if your pre-1986 Camaro has a V-8, it was born with a Q-jet nestled between the valve covers.

GM spent decades developing the Quadrajet 2-stage, air-valve-secondary 4-barrel carburetor into a first-class fuel-metering device. Its small primary venturis provide excellent throttle response and fuel economy at cruise, and the staged, large-diameter air-valve secondary venturis give plenty of wallop on demand. Cfm to cfm, Q-jets routinely provide better fuel economy than comparable Holleys. Nine times out of ten, it's all the carburetor your Camaro needs.

A minor carburetor overhaul can be accomplished with common hand tools, some carb cleaner, compressed air and a rebuild kit. I also recommend having a *Chevrolet Chassis Overhaul Manual* for your Camaro's model year on hand; rebuild kit illustrations are notoriously fuzzy and seem to apply to every oddball carburetor model except yours. Or you can have your Camaro's original carburetor professionally rebuilt to factory standards. Whatever you do, stay away from chain store rebuilt carbs if at all possible.

Tools & Supplies Needed
- Carburetor rebuild kit
- Common socket and wrench set
- Carburetor cleaner
- Needle-nose pliers
- Magnetic-tipped flat-blade screwdriver
- Phillips-head screwdriver
- WD40
- Propane torch
- Loctite 271 and 290
- Throttle-shaft bushings, reamer and driver
- Bolts and nuts (5/16 x 3")

These are built to the lowest common denominator of performance with whatever parts are available at the time; this jet and that metering rod.

Our 82,500-mile project 1973 Z28 was suffering from poor fuel economy, balky cold-start driveability, and was fuel-starved and cutting out during wide-open-throttle bursts lasting more than 5 seconds. We limped and lurched our way to the Carb Shop in Costa Mesa, California, where proprietor, Mike Riley, gave the Camaro's Quadrajet 4MV a thorough going through. Here's what's involved in the overhaul procedure.

2. Four capscrews retain Q-jet to manifold; front two screws are atop the air horn and may be Phillips-head...

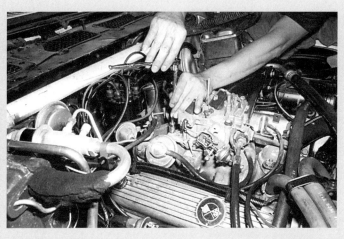

3. ...while two rear hex screws are at base of throttle body. Disconnect fuel inlet with one" flare-nut wrench. Label and disconnect all vacuum hoses.

4. Place Q-jet on wood block to prevent damage to aluminum throttle body and fragile throttle plates. Or make support pedestals using 5/16" bolts and double nuts through carb mounting holes.

5. Q-jet disassembly is straightforward, but take care to first remove these two 8-32 slot-head screws or air horn will be damaged. These hide under choke plate in primary venturi and may be covered by gum and varnish on high-mileage units.

6. The Carb Shop cleans all metal parts in ultrasonic drums filled with heated solvent.

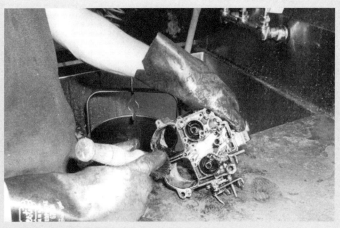

7. At home, a metal or plastic sink, cleaning solvent, a stiff parts-cleaning brush and some elbow grease gets the job done. The three major sections are the air-horn assembly (top), float-bowl assembly (middle) and throttle-body assembly (bottom).

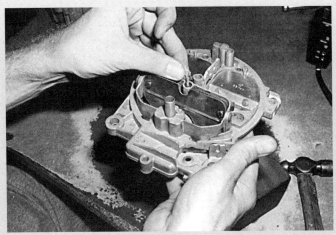

8. If you're a bit of a car klutz, this mod may save you some grief later on. Tap a small tee into the vent hole in air horn. This prevents threading air cleaner stud down through wrong hole and ruining the float.

9. With a light touch, tap emulsion tubes in place on underside of air horn. These tend to loosen in service. Make sure choke plate and secondary air door operate freely with no binding.

10. Quadrajets often leak past lead primary main well plugs (arrow) on underside of float-bowl assembly. Symptoms include an extreme rich condition, poor fuel economy and the float bowl emptying into the manifold if the car sits overnight. To seal these, the Carb Shop first heats them on underside for a few seconds with a propane torch...

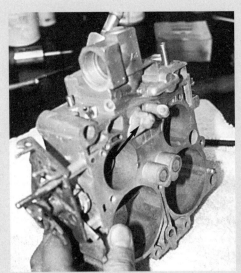

11. ...then, while plugs are still hot, flips over the float bowl and applies a drop or two of self-wicking Loctite 290 (green) directly into each primary main well. The finishing touch is to direct heat once again from a propane torch to the underside of the well plugs

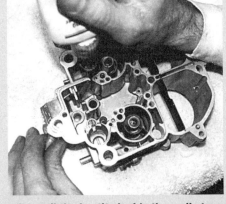

for another 5–8 seconds, until the Loctite inside the wells turns from shiny to dull. Heat too long and the Loctite will crack, and you'll have to start all over again.

12. Leaking problems occur at the large secondary well plugs on the underside of the float-bowl assembly too. Support assembly on wood block and tap each plug using a brass drift about the same size as the plugs. Easy does it; you just want to move the plugs slightly.

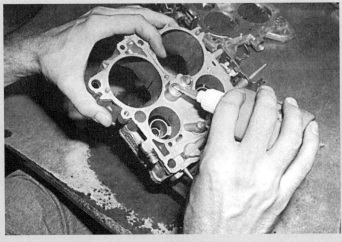

13. Seal the large secondary well plugs by applying green Loctite 290 directly to outside of each plug.

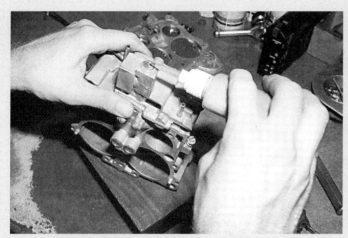

14. Another leak-prone area is the plug alongside the fuel inlet. Put a few drops of green Loctite on it as well.

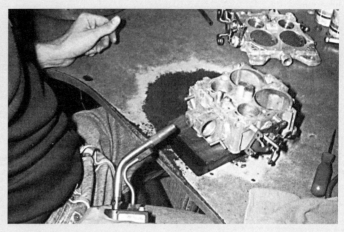

15. Heat the fuel-inlet plug for 5-8 seconds with a propane torch to seal the deal.

17. Line-ream each throttle-shaft bore oversize to accept a 3/8" OD steel bushing.

16. High-mileage Camaros often have a lot of slop and side play where the steel throttle shaft of the primary throttle plates wears away at the softer aluminum throttle body. Symptoms are poor idle quality and tip-in stumble. To fix it, install steel bushings in outboard shaft bores of primaries in throttle body. Throttle plate screws are staked in place. Mark each plate in its matched bore with a magic marker, then grind off the staking with a Dremel tool and remove the screws, plates and shafts. Keep the tiny screws in a Ziploc plastic bag so you don't lose them.

19. Carefully tap in each bushing flush with lip of throttle body. Note how driver pilots in inboard throttle-shaft bore.

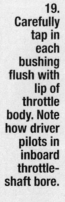

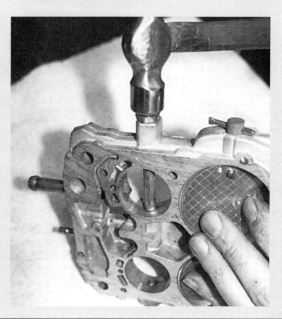

18. Special 5/16" driver is used to install throttle-shaft bushings. Note serrations on OD of bushing (arrow).

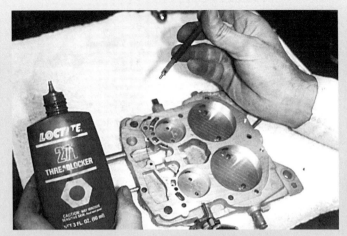

20. Reinstall throttle shafts and plates, using new screws. A magnetic-tip flat-blade screwdriver is a big help here. Apply thread-locking compound (Loctite 271 red or equivalent) to screws.

21. Make sure throttle shafts turn freely and plates do not bind in bores. Check throttle-plate alignment by holding throttle body up to light. Note: number side of throttle plates is facing down.

22. With primary throttles held closed, check for a 0.015–0.020 inch gap between tang and link on secondary throttle arm. Insufficient clearance causes primary throttles to hang open.

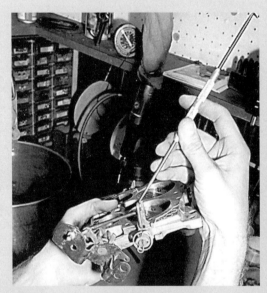

23. If clearance at the secondary throttle arm needs to be adjusted, bend the tang on the primary throttle shaft with needle-nose pliers.

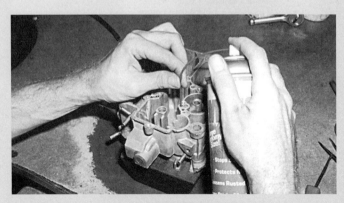

24. After soaking in carb cleaner, blow all float-bowl passages clear with compressed air. NEVER try to remove blockage by running a wire through a passage as the soft aluminum damages easily. Remove stubborn blockages by directing a stream of WD40 through the port until it flows free. Checking idle jets for blockage is a good idea if car sat for a few years and the fuel system dried out or was contaminated.

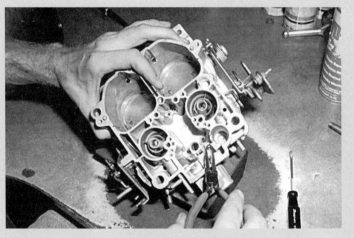

25. Don't lose this large check ball or the accelerator-pump circuit won't function. It hides in a passage under a screw in the float chamber.

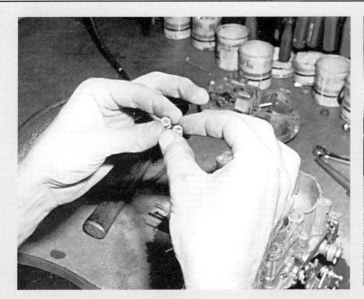

26. Make sure the number codes on the primary jets match as do these #74s. Never drill out jets to increase fuel flow; larger jets are available for that purpose.

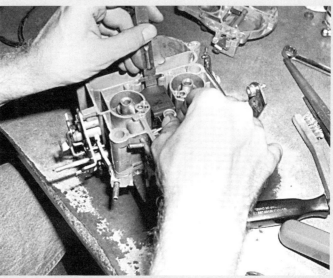

27. Install new needle and seat with a new gasket, then drop float in and hook pull clip from needle and seat onto it. Float level is checked by placing thumb on pivot bar, pushing float up with other finger and measuring from machined surface of float bowl to top of float. Level for this 4MV is 0.25".

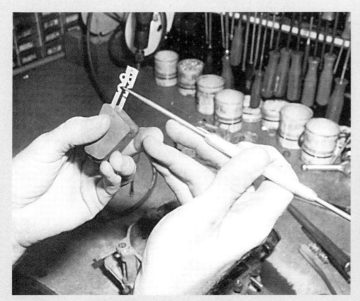

28. Float level is adjusted by opening or closing the V in this tang. Brass floats are best, but Carb Shop says plastic floats are OK if they're the newer, black-color #705 type. Older, brown-color #316 plastic floats were porous and eventually can "sink."

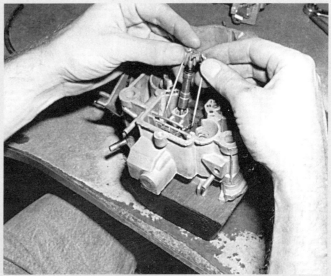

29. Inspect bridge atop power valve to make sure it isn't bowed or bent by previous abuse. Replace if defective. Slide power valve and primary metering rods into their holes and push plastic retaining ring with a screwdriver until it fits flush in power valve bore. When installing air horn, make sure tab on air horn-to-float-bowl gasket slides UNDER metering rod bridge, not over it!

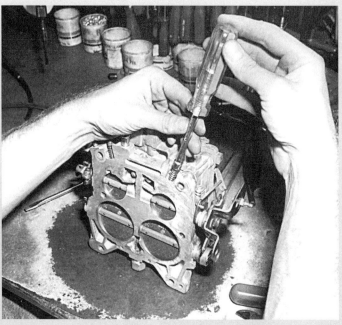

30. There are four different accelerator-pump capacities, ranging from 15cc to 21cc. In a stock rebuild, stick with the factory setting. Use a blue Viton pump seal because it won't be affected adversely by ethanol in today's pump gas. Lube the new seal with WD40, spray some also in the bore and slide in the new accelerator pump. Check that WD40 sprays out the two passage holes when you stroke the pump.

31. Check that the idle mixture screws have sharp tapers. Replace any that are damaged or rounded off. Run the screws all the way in and seat them GENTLY, then back them out each 2–3 turns. This is a good baseline mixture setting.

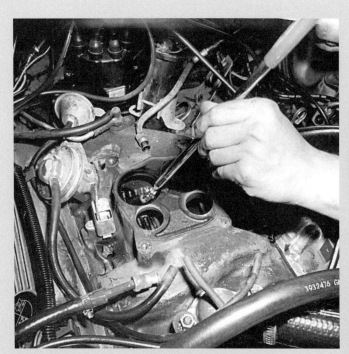

32. Back on the car, it's a good time to clean up the intake manifold and remove deposits while the carb is out.

33. Rebuild complete, it's time to install the Q-jet on our car, hook up the choke rod and vacuum hoses and dial-in the idle mixture on the scope. Always use a new O-ring on the fuel inlet.

Chapter 22

Rebuilding the Muncie Four-Speed

1. To remove the transmission, first remove the shifter boot and unbolt the shifter from the transmission. If your Camaro has a Hurst shifter, this is as simple as removing the two bolts at the base of the shifter.

In the mid to late 1960s, America rediscovered its love affair with the manual transmission. In the Camaro's first few years, more than a third of the ponycars were ordered with manual gearboxes—a much higher percentage on performance models such as the SS350, SS396 and Z28. Similarly, a good number of Novas, Chevelles, Corvettes and even a few Impalas were fitted with four-speeds. Though the cast-iron-case Saginaw four-speed boxes made up a significant portion of the total, the aluminum-case Muncie four-speed was the performance-car buyer's gearbox of choice.

As Detroit's horsepower race began to accelerate in the early 1960s, the venerable Borg-Warner T-10 4-speed that Chevy had used in the Corvette and other applications since the late 1950s couldn't handle the torque output of the newer engines. So GM went back to the drawing board and came up with a heavy-duty in-house design to be built at its Muncie, Indiana, transmission plant.

The first Muncie four-speeds began appearing in GM muscle cars midway into the 1963 model year. Those first few years, the Muncie four-speed was available in two versions: an M-20 wide-ratio box with a 2.52:1 first gear and an M-21 close-ratio version with a 2.20:1 first. Late in the 1965 model year, an extra heavy-duty M-22 version with Low-hclix-angle gears (21-degree pitch versus the M-20's quieter 39-degree gears) was introduced. Dubbed the "rock crusher" due to its characteristic coarse-sounding gear whine, the M-22's extra torque capacity made it the choice of street-racers and drag-racers alike.

It's nearly impossible to find a Muncie four-speed in a junkyard today, but you can still find one at auto swap meets now and then. The rare M-22 rock crusher will cost about three times as much as a used M-20 or M-21. And most of these you'll find will be in need of some maintenance and repair, if not a complete rebuild.

The 1963–65 M-20 and M-21 Muncies are extremely rare and less durable due to their smaller countershaft and narrower synchronizer rings. Unless you're doing a letter-perfect restoration, opt for a 1966-or-later box for a Muncie with more muscle.

GM raised the durability bar a few notches more in 1971 and switched to fine-spline input and output shafts. You can retrofit one of these boxes in an earlier car by swapping to a 1971-or-later clutch disc and Turbo 400 style driveshaft slip yoke.

Identification Tips

Here are a few identification tips to help you figure out what kind of Muncie you're dealing with. Check the diameter of the countergear pin. A 7/8" pin indicates a 1963–65 box and a one-inch pin goes with a 1966–74 Muncie. With that info, start counting the rings on the input shaft. On 1963–65 models, no ring indicates a wide-ratio M-20 while one ring means you have a close-ratio M-21. From 1966 on, the ring ID system changes: No ring gets you an M-22 rock crusher, one ring still nets a close-ratio M-21, and two rings indicates a wide-ratio M-20.

You should also know that input and output shaft spline count changes in 1971. All 1963–70 Muncies have coarse (10 count) input shaft splines, 1971–74 boxes feature fine (26 count) front splines. At the rear, 1963–70 Muncies have small-diameter (27 count) output shaft splines, and 1971–74 boxes get the large-diameter (32 count) shaft. The latter is also known as a Turbo Hydra-matic 400 slip-yoke type, and was first used in a few big-block 1970 Chevelles.

Also, all 1970-and-later Muncies feature a drain plug, while earlier boxes (except the M-22) only have a fill plug. With a drain plug, periodic transmission oil changes are much easier.

To get the lowdown on performance-building the Muncie four-speed to last, we went to Ron's Transmission Service in Garden Grove, California. Proprietor Ron Worthen has been rebuilding Muncies (as well as Saginaw, Borg-Warner T-10 and Super T-10 boxes) for decades.

If at all possible, it's best to rebuild the transmission that came with the car so you know what you're working with. Our project '67 Camaro RS reached its fifth owner with a freshly built 275-hp 327 4-bbl, but the trans (a 1970-vintage M-20) was noisy and jumping out of second gear on coast-down. These are clues that can help identify problem areas and worn parts later on teardown.

In addition to the normal replacement items such as gaskets, seals, bearings, rear bushing, springs, keys and synchros, Ron usually replaces the 1–2 and 3–4 speed clutch sliding sleeves, the front bearing retainer and its locknut, the reverse idler gear and countergear shaft.

GM no longer stocks most of the parts for the Muncie, so if any of the gears or other major hard parts need to be replaced, you're looking at chasing down used parts or buying new aftermarket pieces, many of which are imported. Quality varies widely.

As the trans comes apart, check for worn parts that offer clues to past abuse. Synchro ring teeth wear is normal, so a small amount of "brass" in the trans lube

or stuck to the drain-plug magnet is normal. Spin the main drive and mainshaft ball bearings. Noisy bearings as well as worn thrust washers indicate a trans that was run hot or low on gear lube. Excessive input shaft side play or end play, or a twisted input shaft or mainshaft points to extreme (and probably repeated) driveline shock. A chewed reverse slider gear results from shifting to reverse while the car is moving forward. Other ham-fisted damage includes work shift forks or bent detent cams in the side cover from over-enthusiastic speed shifting.

High-mileage cars most often suffer a worn front bearing retainer due to throwout bearing friction. This can cause clutch release to be notchy. Likewise, a worn third gear sleeve will allow the trans to pop out of gear. Check the fit of the countershaft pin in the case. The slightest slop here will cause a gear lube leak.

Room doesn't permit us to detail every teardown and rebuild step. Besides, that's what a Chevy overhaul manual is for. Follow along as Ron Worthen imparts some important tips on building a Muncie four-speed to last.

2. Jack up the car at least two feet and install jack stands under the front subframe and rear spring perches. Unbolt the rear U-joint and slide the driveshaft out of the transmission. If you have a spare slip yoke, slide it back into the transmission to keep it from leaking gear lube.

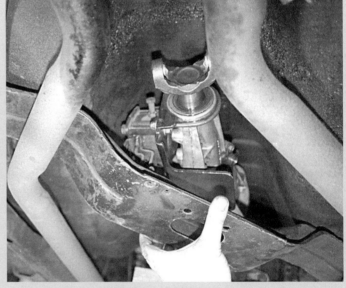

3. Support the engine oil pan with a floor jack cushioned with a wooden block. Unbolt the transmission from its rear mount. If you have a standard Muncie or Saginaw shifter, unbolt the strut rod from the transmission and the shifter from the crossmember. Remove the four crossmember-to-body bolts and nuts, angle the crossmember diagonally and slide it out. Check clearance between the ignition distributor and the firewall. If the exhaust system is hooked up, clearance shouldn't be a problem. But if the exhaust is disconnected, be careful not to tilt the engine so far rearward that the distributor is damaged.

4. If you don't already have some, fabricate a set of four guide studs by hacksawing the heads off some 1/2x13x4" coarse-thread bolts. Cut slots in them so they can be installed and removed with a flat-blade screwdriver.

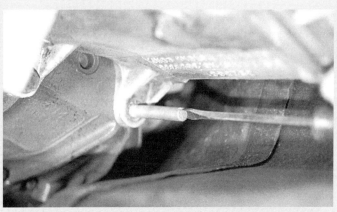

5. Remove two of the four transmission-to-bellhousing bolts and install two of the guide studs using a screwdriver. This will keep the transmission from damaging the clutch and/or you when it lowers as you remove the last of the four bolts.

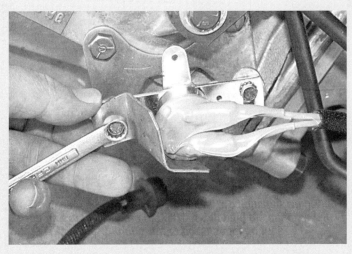

6. Disconnect the back-up lamp switch at the transmission.

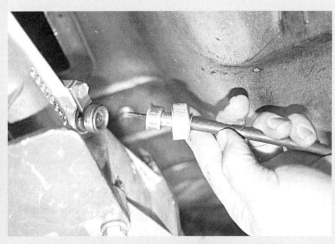

7. Disconnect the speedometer at the transmission.

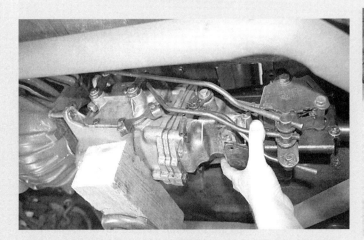

8. With the transmission supported by a second floor jack and steadied by an assistant, slide the transmission downward and rearward, off the guide studs. Lower the jack and the transmission to the floor.

9. Place the transmission over a drain pan, remove the drain plug (or fill plug on early Muncies) and drain the gear lube out of the transmission.

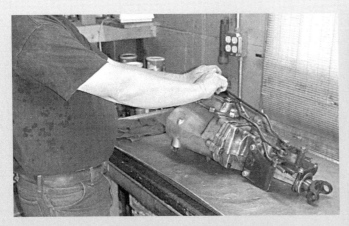

10. Select a clean, well-lit area to disassemble the transmission. You'll be dealing with hundreds of parts, many of them very small, so good organization is key to success. Start disassembly by removing the linkage and shifter mechanism.

11. Remove the side-cover bolts and pull off the side cover. Make sure the detent cams and levers are straight and not worn.

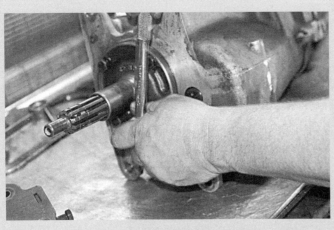

12. At the front, check the side play and end play on the input shaft. Straighten the lock tabs for the front bearing retainer bolts and remove the bolts. Tap the retainer with a plastic hammer and slide it off the input shaft.

13. To loosen or tighten main drive locknut, put trans in two gears at once (reverse and fourth). Note left-hand threads on locknut which are opposite normal rotation; go clockwise to loosen it. Input shaft on this M-20 was visibly twisted from previous driveline abuse. Remove the locknut and check the condition of the large ball bearing directly behind it.

14. Put trans in neutral and drive out lock pin from bottom of reverse-gear shift-lever boss.

15. Thread a shift-lever bolt into the reverse shift fork and pull it out slightly to disengage the fork from reverse gear.

16. Remove the six extension-housing bolts. Using a plastic hammer, tap on the reverse shift-lever bolt toward the rear, disengage the reverse fork from reverse gear and remove the extension housing. Remove the reverse idler gear, shaft, flat thrust washer and lock pin. Depress the retaining clip and slide off the speedometer drive gear and reverse gear.

17. Slide the 3-4 synchro sleeve into fourth gear. Using a plastic hammer tap rearward on the rear bearing retainer and pull out the mainshaft gear assembly.

18. Now strip the case. Lift out the front half of the reverse idler gear and its thrust washer. Strip the needle rollers and fourth gear synchro ring from the main drive and press or tap the main drive out from the front of the case. From inside the case, tap out the front ball bearing and retaining ring. Then from the front again, press or drive out the countergear and remove its tanged washers. Unload the 112 needle bearings (80 in 1963–65 transmissions) and four spacers from inside the countergear.

19. With snapping-ring pliers, spread the rear bearing retainer snap ring and drive the mainshaft out of the retainer using a plastic hammer.

20. Remove the mainshaft snap ring and slide third and fourth speed clutch assembly, third speed gear and its synchronizer ring from the front of the mainshaft.

21. Remove the mainshaft rear snap ring. While supporting second speed gear, tap the rear of the mainshaft on a wooden block as shown to loosen items remaining on shaft. These include the rear bearing, first speed gear and sleeve, first speed synchro ring, one-two speed synchronizer clutch assembly, second speed synchro ring and second gear.

22. Both third and second gears can usually be installed/removed using a hammer and brass drift, but first gear is best pressed on and off using a hydraulic press.

23. Now is a good time to replace the extension-housing bushing. You can cut the old one out with a chisel or drift pin, but the new bushing must be installed with a bushing driver.

24. Fresh out of the cleaning tank, inspect and organize all parts for assembly. Take an inventory of all parts, large and small, before starting the rebuild.

25. Trans ID on 1966-74 Muncies is as easy as counting input shaft rings. Left to right: M-22 rock crusher (no ring), M-20 wide-ratio (2 rings) and M-21 close-ratio (one ring).

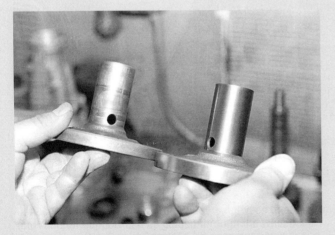

26. On high-mileage cars, throwout bearing wears grooves in bearing retainer, left. Routinely this part is replaced to avoid clutch problems down the road.

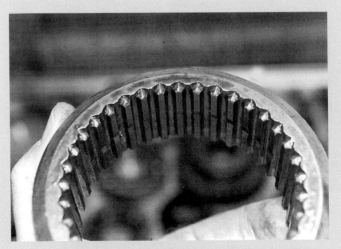

27. Inner splines on clutch sliding sleeve should have sharp "points" and not be rounded off.

28. Normal replacement parts in a Muncie rebuild include new synchros, ball bearings, needle bearings, rear bushing and seal, plus all keys, snap rings, spacers, gaskets, and O-rings.

29. Experienced trans builders like Ron Worthen check fit of new brass synchro rings on gear hubs by feel. After lubing, synchro should rotate smoothly in one direction and provide brake action in the other. Twist and feel for high spots. If you're replacing synchro rings, try different combinations until you find a good match. Install all three synchro rings this way.

30. From rear of mainshaft, slide on second gear assembly with hub toward rear of shaft until it butts against step near front of shaft. This will start your mainshaft gear stack.

31. Using new keys, install 1-2 clutch hub in 1-2 clutch sliding sleeve and secure in place with new snap rings (key springs) on both sides, taper side up. Snap rings must cover keys.

32. Slide the 1-2 clutch assembly on the rear of the mainshaft, taper to the rear and hub to the front, and drive it on with a 1-3/4" ID pipe and a brass drift.

33. Go for 0.050–0.070" between the brass synchro ring and gear engagement teeth of first gear assembly.

34. Slide on first gear assembly from rear of mainshaft with hub toward front. Then install rear ball bearing atop first gear and slam mainshaft onto work table to seat bearing. Drive bearing on with drift and 1-5/8" pipe if necessary.

35. Using snap-ring pliers, install a new snap ring in groove behind rear bearing. There should be no more than 0.005 inch clearance between snap-ring and bearing. Oil bearing and spin to make sure it isn't noisy or galled.

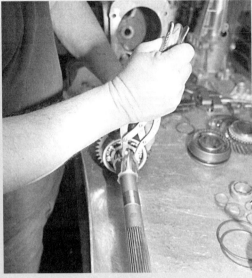

36. Slide on third gear assembly from front of mainshaft with hub to the front. Then assemble the 3-4 clutch hub and sliding sleeve with new keys and snap-rings (key springs) just as you did for the 1-2 clutch assembly. Slide the 3-4 clutch assembly onto the front of the mainshaft with sleeve taper and hub toward the front and keys in hub matching with notches in third gear synchro ring. Install snap-ring in groove in front of mainshaft against 3-4 clutch assembly.

37. Insert a new snap-ring inside the rear bearing retainer, slide the retainer on the shaft and with snap-ring pliers, engage the snap-ring into the groove in the rear bearing.

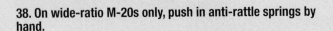

38. On wide-ratio M-20s only, push in anti-rattle springs by hand.

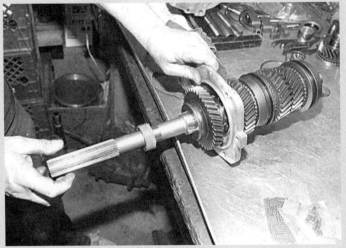

39. Slide on reverse gear (shift collar to rear) and speedometer gear with retaining clip to front. The mainshaft is now done.

40. On 1966-74 Muncies, a total of 112 of these needle bearings support the countergear in four sets of 28, separated by spacers. These are coated with grease and loaded from the rear using a dummy shaft. Lose just one of these and it'll be a long day. And don't even think about trying to put the needle bearings in without the dummy shaft.

41. Here's the last of six spacers, with the 112 needle bearings loaded inside.

42. Coat the countershaft's front and rear tanged thrust washers with grease and install them in the case. Slide in countergear.

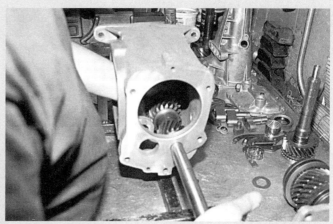

43. While supporting countergear in place, drive countershaft in through front of case, displacing dummy shaft. Make sure countershaft notch is parallel to ground and relieved step is on bottom. Take care not to knock tanged thrust washers loose.

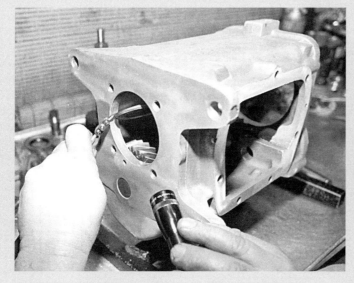

44. Check front and rear of case to make sure tanged thrust washers index properly using a flashlight and small mirror.

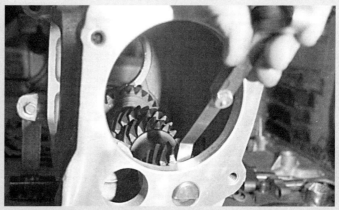

45. Countergear pin diameter identifies box as a 1963–65 (7/8") or 1966–74 (one inch) unit. For optimum performance, keep countershaft end play in the 0.010-0.015" range. Up to 0.025" is allowable. Spin cluster shaft and listen for fallen needles or metallic bearing noise that would spell disaster.

46. Coat 17 roller bearings with grease, install in cage and place bearing assembly into main drive gear.

47. Install fourth gear synchro ring on the main drive gear with notches facing rear of transmission. Position main drive over snout of mainshaft, engaging notches in fourth gear synchro with keys in clutch assembly. Tap third/fourth gear sliding sleeve forward into fourth gear position which holds the assembly together.

48. Place new gasket on front of rear bearing retainer. Coat the tanged washer and front reverse idler gear with grease and install the thrust washer and idler gear in the machined cavity in the rear of the case. Then load mainshaft into case, supporting it from side cover opening. With rear bearing retainer aligned with pin, tap assembly flush with rear of case.

49. Install the rear reverse idler gear, engaging the splines in the front reverse idler gear. Then install second thrust washer on the reverse idler shaft, tap shaft into case so it engages front thrust washer and install roll pin in vertical position.

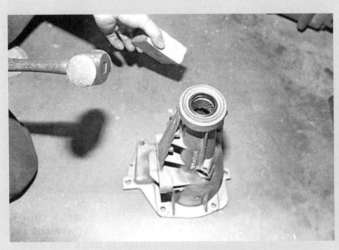

50. Install new rear bushing and lip seal in extension housing, then check fit by inserting driveshaft slip yoke.

51. Install a new lip seal in the reverse shifter shaft bore.

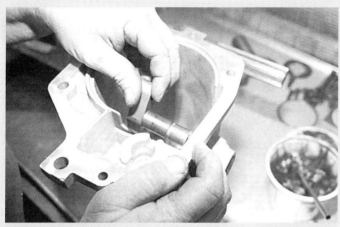

52. Use an offset screwdriver to depress spring-loaded detent ball to install reverse shifter shaft in extension housing.

54. Push or pull reverse shifter shaft to align groove in shaft with hole in housing and tap in roll pin.

56. Install front bearing retainer (easy if you have three hands) with a new gasket and lock strips. Make sure oil hole is at bottom. Torque four bolts to 22 ft-lb and bend lock-strip tabs against bolt slats to secure them.

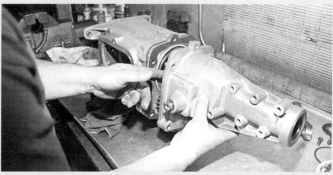

53. Coat with grease and install a new gasket on the rear of the rear bearing retainer. Then start extension housing onto the case while pushing in the shifter shaft to engage the shift fork with the reverse gear collar. Pilot the reverse idler shaft into the extension housing as it butts against the case. Install six extension housing bolts; the longer bolts go in the bottom. It's a good idea to slip the driveshaft slip yoke into the transmission to center the extension housing. Torque the bolts to 45 ft-lb.

55. Install main drive gear bearing on main drive (input) shaft. Make sure snap ring on gear is installed with groove to the front. Then install the oil slinger with its tangs to the front. Lock the transmission in two gears as you did on disassembly and install the main drive gear retaining nut (note reverse threads). Tighten it to 40 lb-ft and stake it to the retainer with a center punch to prevent it from backing out.

57. Detent cams in side cover are interchangeable, with rounded sides facing each other. Don't get shifter shafts mixed up.

58. To install side cover and forks, first lever trans into second gear as shown.

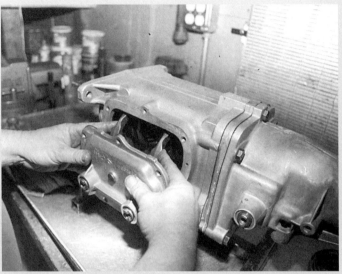

59. Install new lip seals in side cover shifter-shaft holes. When installing side cover, guide forks onto clutch sliding sleeves. Note "nail head" detent cam pivot pin (1969 and later) which are preferable to earlier small-head pin which could pull through side cover and lock trans in two gears. Torque side-cover bolts to 22 ft-lb.

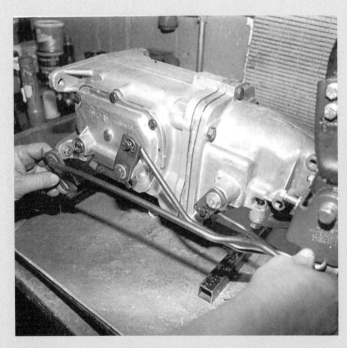

60. Install 1-2, 3-4 and reverse shift levers, shifter and linkage. Completed transmission is ready for installation.

61. Fill transmission with 1.6 pints of 80W/90 gear lube through the filler plug. You can do this in the car, but it's much easier to get at everything now. A small gear-lube pump works best. Install an old driveshaft slip yoke or equivalent in the extension housing to prevent lube from leaking out until you install the driveshaft.

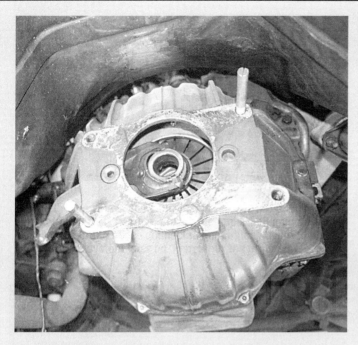

62. Install a pair of guide studs on the bellhousing.

63. With the help of an assistant, raise the transmission on a transmission jack or equivalent, center the input shaft in the clutch throwout bearing and slide the transmission onto the guide studs. Be careful, as the transmission is very heavy.

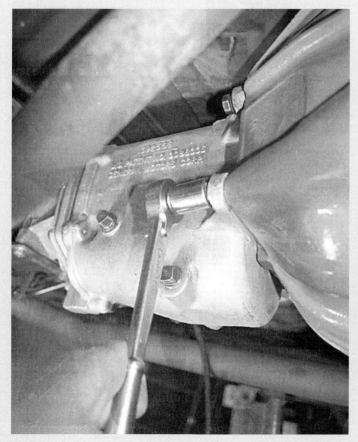

64. Bolt the transmission to the bellhousing and torque to 55 ft-lb. Then connect the speedometer, back-up lamp switch wire, rear mount, crossmember, driveshaft and shifter.

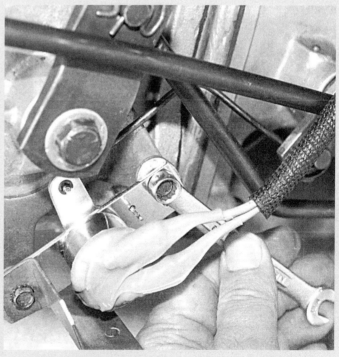

65. Install the back-up light switch, hooking the switch actuating rod into the reverse shifter lever. Adjust position of back-up light switch in bracket by inserting 0.093" drill bit into index hole as shown and tightening mounting screws. Then check for reverse-lamp operation when shifter is placed in reverse.

Chapter 23

Replacing the Clutch

1. Jack up your Camaro to a comfortable working height, about two feet off the ground, if possible. Install sturdy jack stands under the front subframe and rear spring front anchors. Then remove the shifter, disconnect the speedometer and parking-brake cables, clutch-adjusting rod and return spring and backup-lamp switch. Finally, remove the driveshaft, transmission and the crossmember as detailed in the Muncie chapter on page 113.

Like the brakes in your Camaro, the manual-transmission clutch relies on the principle of friction to do its job. The difference is, of course, the clutch is a middleman, helping to get your Camaro under way, while the brakes' mission is to bring things to a halt. The dry-plate clutch used in all stick-shift Camaros is designed to smoothly connect or disconnect the engine's rotating flywheel to the transmission's input shaft. With a manual transmission, the driver controls how gradually or abruptly that happens by depressing or releasing the clutch pedal. The pedal is connected to the clutch throwout (or release) bearing via mechanical linkage. The clutch assembly consists of a steel friction disc with friction material on both sides, sandwiched between the engine-driven cast-iron flywheel and clutch pressure plate that's bolted to the flywheel. The friction disc is splined to the transmission input shaft.

This isn't exactly rocket science, but the linkage must be adjusted with the correct amount of free play for the clutch to function properly, about 1 to 1-1/8". Too little free play and the clutch may slip under load; too much, and gear clash will occur. Adjust free play by loosening the adjusting nuts and lengthening or shortening the threaded rod where the linkage contacts the release fork, then tighten the nuts.

As the years and miles pile on, the friction material on the disc slowly wears away, necessitating periodic adjustment of the linkage. Given normal, non-destructive driving, there's no reason a clutch disc won't last 50,000 miles or more, especially if there's a lot of highway miles involved. On the other hand, if you're hitting the drag strip on weekends, revving the engine to the sweet spot on the power band and side-stepping the clutch, visits to the clutch doctor will be

Tools & Supplies Needed
- Floor jack
- Jack stands
- Socket sets (1/2" and 1/4" drive)
- Open-end wrench set
- Box-end wrench set
- Flex-head 9/16" socket and 12" socket extension
- Oil-filter wrench
- Torque wrench
- Channel-lock pliers
- Clutch-alignment tool
- Fywheel-blocking tool
- Moly grease
- Allen-head driver set
- Flat-blade screwdriver
- Needle-nose pliers

more frequent. Ditto for stop-and-go commuting, although I doubt many 30-year-old Camaros see this kind of daily service these days.

Most clutches get replaced not because their friction material has worn down to the rivets, but because of overheating due excessive and repeated slippage. Not only does heat oxidize the friction material but it also can warp the pressure plate and flywheel. This causes uneven engagement and characteristic "chatter." Also the release bearing can fail due to excessive "riding the clutch" or if the car is swamped in deep water.

Any decades-old Camaro should also have its clutch linkage checked. On early models, this is a system of rods, bellcranks and levers with lots of wear points to deal with. Rubber seals for the linkage at the firewall and bellhousing seal out dirt and noise, but in time dry out and decompose. Slop in the linkage can make precise operation of the clutch very challenging.

If you're going to have a look at the clutch, take the time to service other components in the immediate area. To remove the clutch, you must pull the driveshaft, remove the transmission, starter, oil filter and bellhousing. Add the engine flywheel to that list if clutch chatter is a problem or if the flywheel looks like

it's blued, heat-checked or scored.

It isn't always necessary to replace the clutch pressure plate if disc wear is minimal, but as long as the car is apart it's good insurance to do the job now rather than have to tear the drivetrain apart again a few thousand miles down the road. On the other hand, always use a new throwout bearing upon assembly. And check the condition of the clutch release fork and pivot ball. On a high-mileage Camaro, the ball is likely galled and the spring clip for the throwout bearing is probably sprung. Replace these as necessary.

2. Disconnect the battery cables at the battery. Then disconnect the wires at the starter motor, remove the starter, flywheel inspection plate and oil filter.

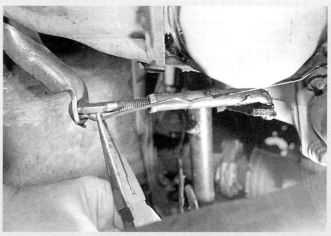

3. Disconnect the clutch linkage return spring at the adjusting rod.

4. Remove the clutch bellhousing bolts. To gain access to the upper bolts against the transmission tunnel, use a long extension and a swivel-head 9/16" socket. When all bolts have been removed, rap on the aluminum bellhousing with a rubber hammer to pop it loose.

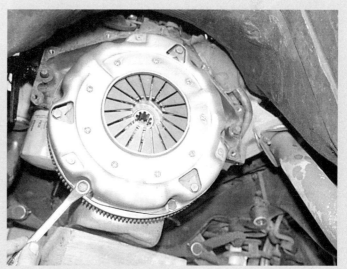

5. Unbolt the clutch pressure plate from the flywheel. As you loosen the last pressure-plate bolt, support underneath as the pressure plate is heavy, and the disc will now slide out. Remove the clutch assembly.

6. Inspect the flywheel. If the clutch is chattering badly or if the flywheel is visibly scored, heat-checked or blued, it should be milled and resurfaced at a machine shop. If it's coming off, first mark its position relative to the crankshaft with paint dots.

7. Flywheel may want to turn as you try to loosen bolts. If this is the case, a commercially available flywheel-teeth-clamping tool like this one from K-D Tools is ideal. Just lock the tool onto the flywheel teeth and rotate the flywheel until the handle of the tool butts up against some thing solid. Then break the bolts loose.

8. Minor wear like this on pressure plate can be cleaned up with crocus cloth. Note radial cross-hatching on friction surface which indicates pressure plate is nearly new.

9. Nevertheless, the previous owner had installed a super-high-effort racing clutch (left) that was very tiring to drive around town. Decision was made to go with new stock clutch assembly from Classic Industries (right) with lower, but entirely adequate, clamping pressure. This is sold as a matched assembly including friction disc, diaphragm-type pressure plate and throwout bearing.

10. While they're removed, clean the bellhousing and flywheel inspection cover with solvent to remove any traces of oil.

11. For a fresh appearance, paint as required. The inspection cover should be semi-gloss engine enamel while the bellhousing is either unpainted aluminum, or Chevy Orange semi-gloss enamel depending on application.

12. If you're planning to reuse the friction disc, inspect it. Discard any disc that's oil-contaminated (from a leaking rear main engine seal), has burned linings or if the lining is worn past the radial grooves (to less than 0.28" thickness when miked in a vise). Also replace a disc if you can spin any of its five damping springs.

13. Likewise, the pressure plate can be reused provided its pressure ring is free of scoring and heat damage. Check for warpage with a straightedge, and discard the pressure plate if it exceeds 0.010". If reusing, clean with solvent.

14. Slide the clutch fork off its pivot ball in the bellhousing and inspect both for wear. Replace fork if bent, worn or if spring clip doesn't clamp securely to pivot ball. Don't reuse pivot ball if worn or galled as shown in example (left).

15. If necessary, replace clutch fork pivot ball using a large Allen wrench. Apply a coating of moly grease to the ball for assembly.

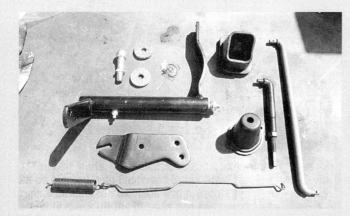

16. Mechanical clutch linkage was sloppy and showing lots of wear, so we replaced it with this small-block V-8 kit from Year One, Inc., complete with all rods, levers, rubber boots, clips, brackets, washers, pivot bar and spring. All you add is some grease.

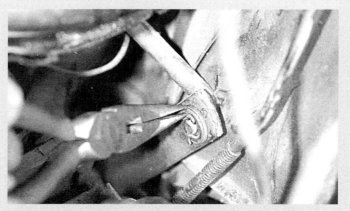

17. Linkage is buried in hard-to-access space between toe board, inner wheelhouse, subframe and brake master cylinder. It comes apart by removing these spring clips with needle-nose pliers. Loosen the nut on the outboard end of the pivot bar, angle the bar downward and pull it off its engine pivot ball.

18. Slip a new rubber boot on the long rod connecting the clutch pedal to the pivot bar. The boot attaches to the engine side of the firewall with two small hex screws.

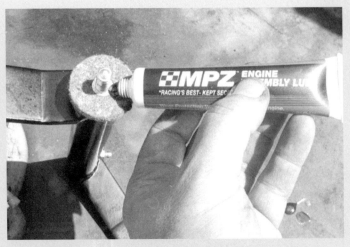

19. Assemble the new pivot bar using new felt washers and moly lube.

20. Then pump 5–6 shots of grease into it through the grease nipple.

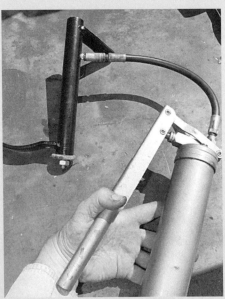

21. Coat the engine pivot ball with moly grease and slide the pivot bar onto it.

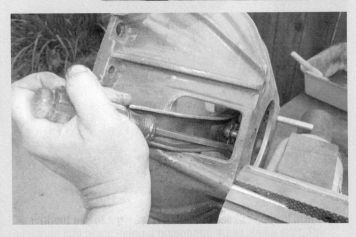

22. Slide the outboard pivot-bar bracket onto the bar, tighten the pivot-bar nut and bolt the bracket to the subframe.

23. Meanwhile, back at the bellhousing, slide the clutch fork back onto the pivot ball. With a new fork and ball, this will be a tight fit; use a long screwdriver if necessary to help spread open the fork's spring clip and guide it onto the ball.

24. Then install the rubber fork-to-bellhousing seal.

25. If flywheel was removed, check for oil leakage at rear main seal—a Chevy small-block V-8 bugaboo. This repair is detailed in *How to Rebuild Your Small-Block Chevy* by HPBooks.

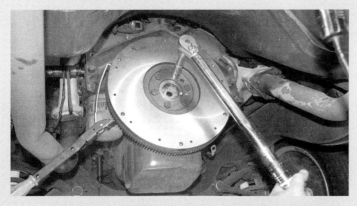

26. Install flywheel, matching the marks you made earlier. Use the flywheel-teeth-clamping tool if necessary and tighten the flywheel bolts in a crisscross pattern to 60 ft-lb.

27. Assemble the friction disc and pressure plate, making sure this side of disc faces flywheel as shown.

28. Loosely install pressure-plate bolts. This next step is important: Insert a clutch-disc alignment tool into the assembly until it bottoms out in the crankshaft pilot bearing. While supporting and centering the tool, tighten the pressure plate bolts in a crisscross pattern to 35 ft-lb. If you don't get this exactly right, the transmission input shaft won't slide into the clutch and you'll have to align the disc all over again. (We did, three times!)

29. Slip the throwout bearing onto the clutch fork and offer up the bellhousing to the engine. Tighten bellhousing bolts to 30 ft-lb. Remember, it's aluminum!

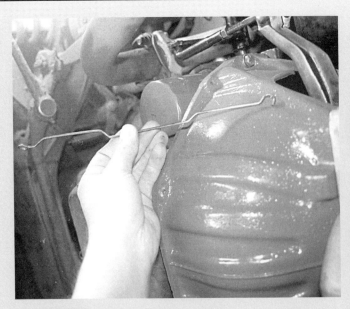

30. Install the remainder of the clutch linkage and connect to the release fork. Note special long spring on early small-block Camaros that connects to left engine mount.

31. Install the inspection cover, starter, oil filter and connect the starter wires and positive battery cable. Then install the transmission as detailed in the Muncie section, page 113.

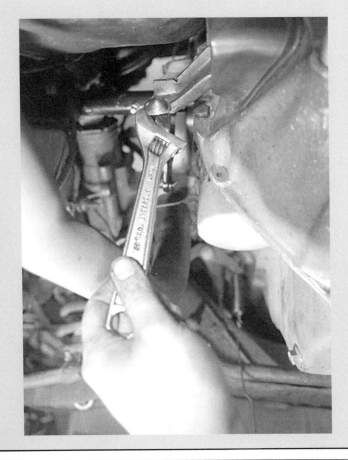

32. Finally, adjust clutch freeplay by lengthening or shortening threaded adjusting rod at release fork. Maintain 1- to 1-1/8" freeplay at pedal.

Chapter 24

Installing a Hurst Shifter

1. First step to removing the floppy factory shifter is removing the shifter plate, boot and trim ring from the console or transmission tunnel.

It's a rare aftermarket product that makes it onto the General Motors assembly line, but starting in the late 1960s, the Hurst Competition Plus shifter played a key role in GM's performance-car image. The Hurst floor shifter was factory-installed in all 1969 Camaros with the M-20, M-21 or M-22 Muncie transmission and made other appearances in subsequent General Motors muscle cars of the era.

In the late 1950s and early 1960s, America had rediscovered the joy of manual gearboxes, often teamed with ever-more-powerful V-8 engines. George Hurst built a reputation for building strong, lightweight, precision-feel aftermarket floor shifters that could be substituted for the often clunky, vague column shifters that came in many of Detroit's sedans of the time. Even when the Motor City began fitting four-speed floor shifters in its performance-oriented models, the Hurst shifter reigned supreme as a popular replacement item for street and strip.

A case in point is our project '67 Camaro RS with L30 275-hp 327 V-8. Over the years, the original Saginaw cast-iron-case four-speed was replaced by a '70 Muncie aluminum-case M-20 wide-ratio four-speed and the shifting

Tools & Supplies Needed
- Socket set (3/8" drive)
- Open-end wrench set
- Phillips-head screwdriver
- Floor jack and wood block
- Pair of sturdy jack stands

action of the factory linkage had become sloppy and imprecise. The factory floor shifter bolts to the transmission crossmember and is stabilized by a long, rubber-isolated strut rod affixed to a bracket at one of the transmission's extension-housing-to-case bolts. When driven hard, the shifter flexes and the feel is less than satisfactory. The Hurst unit, on the other hand-clamps securely to the transmission, so flex is almost non-existent. And the Hurst's close tolerances and lightweight shift rods make it a willing accomplice, whether just cruising the strip or engaging in more enthusiastic driving.

2. Jack up the car a good 1-1/2 to 2 ft and place jack stands under the front subframe. To remove the stock Saginaw/ Muncie four-speed shifter shown here, first unbolt the 1-2, 2-4 and reverse shifter arms from the side of the transmission, and the shifter strut rod from the extension-housing-to-case flange. Then unbolt the shifter mechanism from the transmission crossmember and lower the shifter mechanism out of the car. Keep the shifter arms and rods with the shifter.

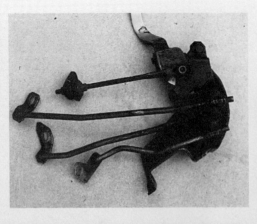

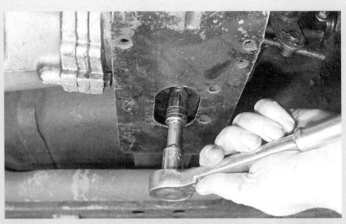

3. Unbolt the rubber transmission mount from the crossmember, then from the transmission. With a floor jack and wood block, jack up the transmission slightly so it's raised off the mount. Remove the mount for the time being.

4. Shifter was installed with transmission on bench for sake of better photos, but it's just as easy to do it in-car. Position new Hurst mounting bracket and temporarily install (but do not tighten) trans-mount-to-bracket bolts.

5. Fasten U-bolt around rear of extension housing and tighten nuts.

6. Mount Hurst shifter on bracket with two bolts. Rear bolt hole is slotted to allow fore/aft tilt for different console configurations. For now, position rear bolt in middle of slotted hole and tighten mounting bolts.

7. Using new nylon bushings and spring clips, assemble shifter rods to their respective transmission arms.

8. Run Hurst rod-adjusting buttons onto shifter rods to midpoint on threads. Also, insert nylon bushings into holes in levers at base of shifter.

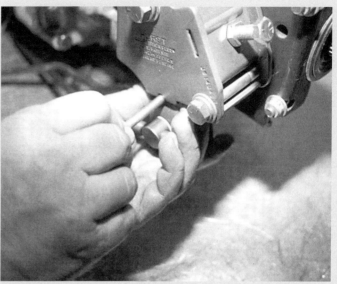

9. Align all three levers at bottom of shifter and insert neutral alignment rod as shown through notch in shifter frame and through holes in three levers. Slip shifter end of all three rods into nylon bushings.

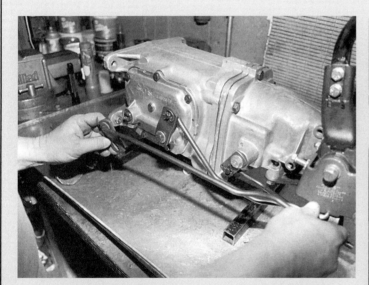

10. Rotate 1–2 and 3–4 transmission arms back and forth through full travel to find neutral position, which should be midpoint. Then adjust length of 1–2 rod and 3–4 rod by spinning them in their buttons and install arms on transmission with stock nuts and washers. For the reverse rod, move the arm fully forward (to the disengaged position) to install. Once all rods are adjusted, fasten them to the shifter with spring clips.

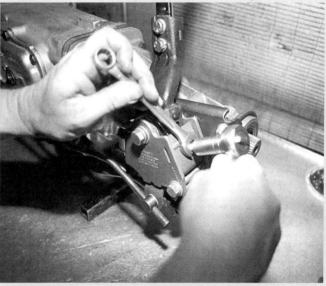

11. Remove the neutral alignment rod and check shifter operation. It should move freely side to side in neutral. Check shifter arms for full engagement of all forward speeds and reverse. Install shifter stop bolts and locknuts by turning them in just a few threads. Place shifter into third gear and screw in stop bolt on rear of shifter until contact is made, then back out stop bolt one full turn and tighten locknut. Repeat for fourth gear by placing shifter in fourth gear and adjusting stop bolt on front of shifter in same manner.

12. If you haven't already done so, reinstall rubber transmission mount on shifter mounting bracket and tighten hex screws into transmission. Then lower transmission onto crossmember and install mount to crossmember.

13. Remove the jack stands and lower the car. On top, bolt the shifter handle to the shifter mechanism using the two bolts and combined threaded nut provided.

14. And there you have it: a shifter that looks better and outperforms the original by far.

BRAKES, CHASSIS
&
SUSPENSION

Chapter 25
Brake Rebuild

1. Perhaps the most important mechanical component of your Camaro is its brake system. Before pulling off any wheels, make sure the car is securely supported on jack stands. Never go under a car that's supported only by a floor jack.

If you do nothing else to your Camaro, at least make sure the brake system is functioning as it should. Looking good and going fast is fun, but all of that fun can come to an ignominious end if you can't get your Camaro stopped when you have to.

On a 20- to 30-year-old car that's seen hard service (or virtually no service!) and perhaps a series of over-enthusiastic drivers during its life, the brake system may hold some nasty surprises. Don't think you're going to throw in a new set of linings and be done with it. The three main bugaboos are excessive wear, leaking seals and corrosion.

The major wear points of your Camaro's brake system (aside from the linings) are the disc brake rotors and drums where they contact the brake linings. Because the brakes work by converting kinetic energy (your Camaro's forward or rearward motion) into heat energy via friction, the replaceable linings, as well as cast-iron drums and rotors, get worn down a little each time they're used.

Over time, the drums and rotors become too thin to function as reliable heat sinks, and they must be replaced. Perhaps someone wore down the linings completely, and the steel backing plates have scored and gouged the rotors or drums. Or in rust-belt areas, an inactive car may develop a sizable rust ridge at the outer edge of the drum or rotor friction area. Also, sometimes the drums or rotors warp when exposed to excessive heat and cause a brake-pedal pulsation.

If there is sufficient metal thickness remaining, the drums or rotors can be machined or surfaced to establish a smooth friction surface for the linings. Check rotor thickness with an outside micrometer and drum inner diameter with calipers. On most Camaros, the wear limit is cast directly into the rotor or drum in the lugnut area.

Your Camaro really has two brake systems: the parking brake which mechanically applies the rear brakes and the service brakes, which hydraulically apply the brakes at all four wheels. Hydraulic brakes have the advantage of generating a great amount of braking force at the wheels with very little effort at the brake pedal. But like anything else hydraulic, the seals keeping fluid in and air out eventually wear or dry out, causing leaks, loss of pressure and air in the system. Also, over time, glycol-based (DOT 3 and DOT 4) brake fluid absorbs water moisture from the air and becomes corrosive to the brake pistons, cylinders and calipers.

Glycol-based brake fluid should be flushed out and replaced every five years or so, but few people do it. An alternative is silicone-based brake fluid, but it doesn't have the high-temperature durability of glycol-based fluid and the entire brake system must be drained and flushed out with alcohol before switching over to it.

So if you're diving into your Camaro's brakes for the first time and you don't know its service history, expect anything. You'll want to establish a baseline for brake-system performance. If the car is in good running shape and the brakes are functional, the elements of a basic service include new linings, resurfaced drums and rotors, inspection of caliper and wheel-cylinder piston dust boots and seals, lubrication and adjustment of parking-brake linkage, inspection of all three rubber flex hoses (one at each front wheel and one at the rear differential), adjustment of the rear linings and bleeding the brakes, if necessary.

On the other hand, if you just towed a treasure home that sat in a barn for ten years, or if the hydraulic system has been opened or run dry, the ante just got raised. Expect to rebuild or replace the master cylinder, disc-brake calipers and drum-brake wheel cylinders. Also plan on replacing all three flex hoses; old, cracked ones may leak or collapse internally, blocking fluid flow. Some of the steel brake lines could be seriously corroded, chewed up, collapsed or missing; replacements are available from Camaro parts houses in kits. I like to use new brake hardware whenever possible, especially on drum brakes with multitudinous springs. Sometimes you'll wish you had three hands trying to move all the springs, shoes, bellcranks and such into position.

You'll also want to disassemble, clean and lubricate the parking-brake linkage, self-adjusting mechanism and star wheel at each rear drum brake. This takes patience and requires organization. I often leave one side assembled as the other is disassembled so I have a frame of reference.

It's a good idea to inspect, lube and adjust the front wheel bearings, too. If you are removing the front rotors on 1969–81 Camaros for resurfacing or replacement, you must pry off the dust cap, pull the cotter pin, unscrew the castellated nut and remove the outer front wheel bearing anyway. On 1967–68 models with front disc brakes and 1967–69 Camaros with front drums, it's not necessary to pull the front bearings, as the rotors or drums are not integral with the hubs. But have a look anyway. Clean the bearing and check for damaged rollers by spinning them by hand. The inner front wheel bearing hides behind a grease seal on the inboard end of the drum or rotor. To get it out, pry off the grease seal. If all is well, lube both the inner and

outer bearings with bearing grease. Place the inner bearing in position and tap on a new grease seal. Slide the drum or rotor onto the spindle, slip the outer bearing and washer on and install and torque the castellated nut to 12ft-lbs. to seat the bearing. Then, back off the nut until it's just hand tight and align the hole in the castellated nut with the one in the spindle. Use a new cotter pin and replace the dust cap.

Disc brakes are much easier to work on, especially the single-piston caliper type used in the front from 1969 through 1981. To change these pads, just unscrew the two pins, slide out the old pads, lubricate the pins and slide in the new pads. Sometimes you'll have to use a putty knife to push the piston back in its bore enough to fit the new pads. Take care not to tear the caliper-piston dust boot.

That said, disc-brake pistons can pit, corrode and seize in their caliper bores, especially on inactive cars in high-humidity areas. One solution is to sleeve the bores and use stainless-steel pistons. Or switch over to silicone brake fluid.

The four-piston calipers used at the front of 1967–68 cars and some 1969 Camaros with four-wheel discs are very dear to replace these days if they are missing or have seized pistons. But a pad change is as easy as pulling a single pin, rotating the old ones out and the new ones in (with the help of a putty knife). Because there's less clearance there between the rotor and pistons, be sure to install the inboard pads first.

Just maybe you're reacting to a problem with

2. Disc-brake pads are easy to check. These front pads had plenty of meat but a leaking caliper piston contaminated them with brake fluid. On 1967–68 models, pull the cotter pin, and slide out the single retaining pin to access the pads.

3. On 1969–81 disc brakes, unbolt the caliper from the spindle with a 3/8" Allen wrench to get to the pads.

your Camaro's brakes. A metal-to-metal sound should point you in the direction of replacing the linings and resurfacing any scored rotors or drums. A vibration in the steering wheel at speed indicates warped front rotors, and a pulsating pedal may mean an out-of-round drum. A soft pedal or one that goes straight to the floor indicates air in the system or a leak. Look for leakage at each wheel; if none is found, the problem may be a master cylinder that's leaking internally.

If your Camaro has power brakes (most do), it's a conventional setup with intake-manifold vacuum acting on a large diaphragm which reduces pedal effort. Power brakes pretty much work or they don't. If the pedal feels exceptionally hard and the brakes are difficult to apply, either the diaphragm has lost its vacuum supply, is ruptured or the one-way check valve on the diaphragm canister has failed. With a vacuum gauge, check for sufficient vacuum (about 15–20") with the engine running. If OK, ascertain that the check valve holds vacuum. If the check valve is OK, the vacuum booster is likely toast. To remove the booster, you must first unbolt the master cylinder from the firewall, but don't open any of the brake lines or you'll have to bleed the system. There should be enough flex in the steel brake lines to leave them connected.

With the exception of topping off the master cylinder, the brake system must be bled whenever it is opened to replace or service any hydraulic component. Without getting too deep into physics, let's just say that a hydraulic brake system works on the principle that brake fluid cannot be compressed. In a closed system, pressure exerted by the brake pedal causes the master-cylinder piston to move in its bore, which in turn applies pressure on each of the calipers and/or wheel cylinders, causing them to move against the brake linings and the linings against the rotors or drums. Put some air in there and the pedal turns to mush because air is easily compressed.

To bleed air from the hydraulic system, first repair any leaky seals. If fluid can leak out, air can "leak" in. You can either "push" the air out by having an assistant work the brake pedal while you man the bleeder nipples one by one. Or you can "pull" it out with a vacuum pump. The beauty of the vacuum-pump method is that it requires only one person—you. With two people, you tell the assistant to push the pedal to the floor and hold it while you open a bleeder nipple, burp out some air, close the nipple and instruct the pedal-pusher to release the pedal. Do this about ten times for each wheel cylinder or caliper with air in it, starting with the one farthest from the master cylinder. With the vacuum pump, just apply about 25" of vacuum to the nipple, open it, suck out the bad stuff and close the nipple before the dial hits zero. When all you're sucking out is brake fluid and no more bubbles appear, the system is bled. The rest is the same. Note that on 1967–68 Camaros with front disc brakes, it may be necessary to clamp the pressure regulator valve under the master cylinder while bleeding to keep the pressure regulator piston from moving and cutting off pressure to the front wheels.

4. If the front rotors are scored, damage will be easy to spot. If you can catch a fingernail in any of the grooves, the rotor needs to be resurfaced. Mike the rotor to see if it has enough meat left. If not, the rotor must be replaced.

5. Many rotors and drums have the acceptable minimum thickness specification cast into them in the lugnut area. This rotor miked at just under one inch, so it can be resurfaced without worry.

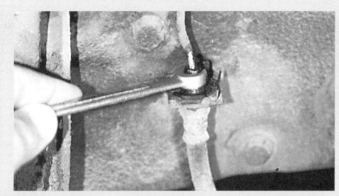

6. When a caliper has to come off, don't let it hang by the flexible rubber hose—that may destroy the hose. Hook the caliper to the subframe with some coat-hanger wire. Or if the caliper pistons need to be serviced, disconnect the steel brake line at the subframe support bracket using a flare-nut wrench. Plug the line to minimize fluid loss.

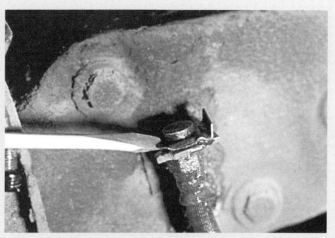

7. Then tap off the spring clip retaining the flex hose to the bracket on the subframe.

8. If you haven't already done so, unbolt the caliper from the spindle.

9. Remove the flex hose from the caliper the same way you did at the subframe. This hose was badly cracked and had collapsed internally, blocking fluid pressure to the caliper pistons.

10. To service the caliper pistons on 1967–68 models, the caliper halves must be separated. Put the caliper in a sturdy vise and get your longest breaker bar. The hex screws holding the caliper halves together are torqued to 130 ft-lb. If necessary, slip a two-foot-long cast-iron pipe over the end of the breaker bar to get more leverage.

11. With caliper halves separated, remove the old piston dust seals by levering up on the inboard lip of the seals with a flat-blade screwdriver using the piston shoulder as a fulcrum. Then lift out the pistons and springs.

12. There are two of these tiny O-rings in each caliper that seal the transfer passage between the two halves. Be sure to install new ones upon assembly or the caliper will leak and not hold pressure.

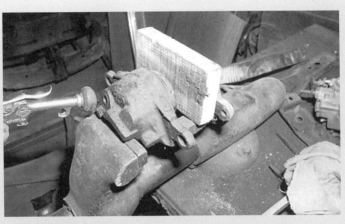

13. On 1969–81 calipers, if the piston is stuck in the bore, you can blow it out using compressed air where the flex hose attaches. Place a wood block in the caliper to cushion the piston as it pops out.

14. Inspect the piston bores. Minor scoring like this is acceptable and can be dressed with a hone. But if you can catch a fingernail on a scoring mark, the caliper needs to be replaced or sleeved.

15. Pull off the old piston seals and discard them.

16. Inspect the pistons. Minor corrosion can be removed with crocus cloth, but large pits may require replacing piston.

17. Items needed to rebuild caliper include seal kit, fresh brake fluid and brake-parts cleaning solvent. Clean the caliper with solvent to remove all traces of grease, road grime, loose rust scale, and old brake fluid. You'll want to coat the piston seals and bores with clean brake fluid later as an assembly lube.

18. Install new piston seals so the lip faces the bore. Help seat the seal in the piston groove by lightly pressing into position with a small, flat-blade screwdriver.

19. Slide the dust seal onto the top of each piston, smear some brake fluid in the bores and gently push the spring and piston assembly into the bore.

20. While applying gentle downward pressure on the piston, work the seal lip into the bore using a thin feeler gauge around its circumference. Use care not to tear the seal.

21. Once the piston is seated in the bore, gently tap each dust seal into the caliper until it sits flush with the top of the bore.

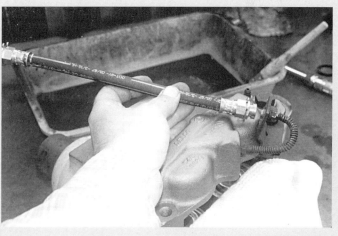

22. For a like-new appearance, spray the calipers with Eastwood Cast Iron Spray Gray.

23. Install a new flex hose on the caliper. First tap in the spring clip retaining it to the bracket, then screw in the steel brake line.

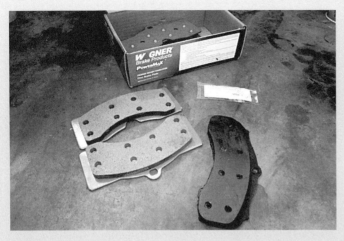

24. Keep the old brake pads to match against the new ones. The first set of pads we ordered (left) did not fit.

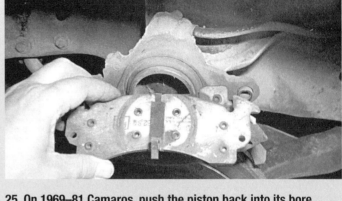

25. On 1969–81 Camaros, push the piston back into its bore with a big C-clamp, install the pad with the clip (shown) on the piston side and the other pad on the opposite side, slip the caliper over the rotor and install the two retaining screws with an Allen wrench. If disconnected, attach the flex hose.

26. On 1967–68 models, it helps to retract the pistons and position the inboard pad inside the caliper as you slip it over the rotor. If left until the end, the inboard pad can be very difficult to install. Then bolt the caliper to the spindle, attach the flex hose, install the outboard pad (using a long screwdriver and putty knife to keep the pistons retracted, if necessary), and finally slide in the brake-pad retaining pin and new cotter key.

27. After sliding the drum off the lugnut studs, take a good look at the layout of the drum-brake assembly before removing anything. For reference take a Polaroid picture or leave one side assembled while you're working on the other one.

28. Bob Baum, of Baum's Auto Supply, measures the drum inner diameter to make sure it hasn't worn beyond specifications.

29. If the drum is scored or out-of-round and has enough meat left, have it machined on a lathe to restore concentricity and surface flatness.

30. After removing any grease, brake fluid or rust, paint the outside of the drum with gloss-black engine enamel for a tough, good-looking finish.

31. Because used drum-brake components are so difficult to work with, I like to go new when I'm restoring a brake system. Laid out for assembly here are new 7/8" wheel cylinders, brake shoes, return springs and shoe anchor pins from Classic Industries.

32. Or if you're on a tight budget, you can try rebuilding the wheel cylinders. Often on old, high-mileage cars, the pistons have to be forced out with compressed air. Note the rusty fluid that dribbled out.

33. This wheel-cylinder bore had a rust ridge and some pitting, but a wheel-cylinder hone cleaned it to a fair degree.

34. Slap some new seals in here, and the system should hold pressure—for a while.

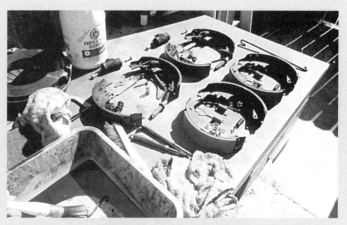

35. Most of the parking brake and self-adjusting hardware for drum brakes will be reused. I like to set up a little assembly line, and as the parts are cleaned, lay them out in position for assembly to avoid confusion.

36. For example, the parking-brake actuating arms are different for the right and left rear brakes. If you look closely, you'll notice the "R" and "L" (shown above) stamped into them.

37. The parking brake itself is a simple three-piece cable. If you're replacing the cable at either rear wheel, push its retainer through the backing plate with a long screwdriver until the four plastic tangs snap into position on the outboard side of the backing plate.

38. During reassembly, here's a case where you might wish you had three hands. Hook the actuating lever on the end of the parking-brake cable, hook the lever on the rear brake shoe with the lever return spring between it and the shoe, hold the anchor-pin washer against the shoe and the anchor pin through the rear of the backing plate...

39. ...then secure the whole shebang to the backing plate with the anchor-pin spring and retainer by rotating it 90 degrees. You may have to try this a few times until you get it right.

40. Apply some Lubriplate grease to the brake-shoe contact points on the backing plate to prevent them from rusting to it.

41. Inspect the adjuster star wheel. If its teeth are chewed up, your Camaro's drum brakes won't self-adjust when they are applied with the vehicle traveling in reverse.

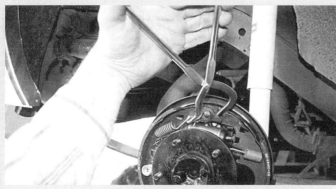

42. Hooking the brake-shoe return springs over the center pivot is a real bear if you don't use the right tools. Always wear safety glasses as a flying spring could injure your eyesight. Some folks swear by these brake-spring tools and others say flat-blade screwdrivers work just as well. Don't expect to get the springs hooked on the first time, every time.

43. When installing the drums, adjust the star wheel until the drum slips on with moderate resistance. Too tight and the drum will drag and overheat the brakes. Too loose and the rear shoes will have too much free play.

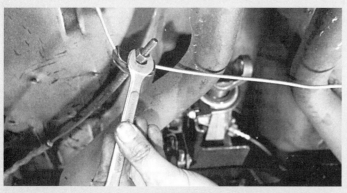

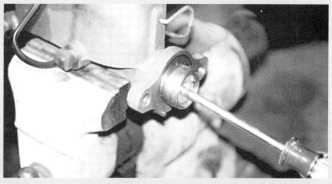

44. When, and only when the rear shoes are adjusted, adjust the center link of the parking brake so it will hold the car on a hill after pressing the parking-brake pedal about an inch.

45. If replacing just the master cylinder, you can bench-bleed it on a vise. This minimizes the need to bleed the cylinders at all four wheels. The bench-bleed kit sold in auto parts stores includes two fittings that thread into the master-cylinder outlet lines, flexible hoses with clips that route back into the reservoirs. Using a long Phillips-head screwdriver, pump the master cylinder pushrod until no bubbles come out of the hoses running into the reservoir.

46. Another big aid when bleeding brakes is a vacuum pump with an air-tight reservoir adapter. Simply attach one hose from the reservoir to the bleeder nipple at the caliper or wheel cylinder and the other hose to the vacuum pump. Squeeze the pump to get 25–30" of vacuum, then crack open the bleeder nipple and suck out the air and aerated fluid. Repeat at each wheel until all air is drawn out.

47. On 1967–68 Camaros with front disc brakes, you must clamp the proportioning valve piston to prevent it from moving during bleeding or the valve will cut off all hydraulic pressure to the front calipers.

Chapter 26

Replacing Subframe Mounts

1. Jack up the car a good 12" or so and place jack stands under the lower control arms and rear axle. NEVER crawl under a car unless it is securely supported on jack stands.

Although the Camaro features a unitized, self-supporting body, it does have a partial front subframe that carries the engine, transmission and front suspension. This partial ladder frame is isolated from the body with six steel-sleeved rubber mounts, or bushings. Each mount consists of two interlocking rubber bushings that capture the subframe. One half fits between the subframe and body or radiator support, while the other goes between the subframe and the mount bolt and large-diameter washer.

In a typical "frame-off" restoration project, the car is completely disassembled and the frame is separated from the body for repair, cleaning, and painting prior to reassembly. Unless it's had mounts replaced already, any 30-year-old Camaro is a candidate for their replacement. But if your Camaro's in decent running shape except for some cracked and decomposed rubber subframe mounts, there is a way to replace them without putting the car in a thousand pieces.

This involves jacking up the car a good 12" or so and placing jack stands under the front-suspension lower-control arms and under the rear axle. With the Camaro so supported you can unbolt the three mounts on one side of the car, keeping the other side assembled so you don't lose the frame's alignment. If the car's been exposed to a lot of road salt, removing these bolts will take a lot of penetrating oil and elbow grease. If the car's rocker panel is in good shape (no serious rust) on that side, you can use its hem flange with the floorpan as a lift point. To do this, place a stout block of wood on a floor jack, position it perpendicular to the front edge of the door, and lift the body only an inch or two, just enough to coax the stuck and rusty mounts out from between the body and subframe. Don't lift the body any higher than this as wires, brake lines, linkages and other parts can only stretch or flex so far.

Tools & Supplies Needed

- Socket set (1/2" drive), long extension, and breaker bar
- Box-end wrenches
- Penetrating oil
- Floor jack and wood block
- Four jack stands
- Subframe mount kit (six two-piece rubber bushings and washers)
- Subframe hardware kit (optional)
- Pry bar or long, stout screwdriver

Then install the new mounts, lower the body onto the subframe and torque the bolts to specifications. After that, move the floor jack and wood block to the opposite rocker panel and replace the other three mounts. Tighten the rear mounts to 75–95 ft-lb and the radiator-support mounts to 30–40 ft-lb.

The forward pair of mounts holds the radiator support to the subframe, and the bolts drop in from the top. To gain access, remove the battery and battery tray and the windshield washer reservoir. The mount under the battery typically is the most rusted, so hit it with a lot of juice and don't rush the job. You'll need your biggest breaker bar for this one. The other four mounts bolt in from the bottom and don't present as much of a challenge.

If the car slips off the jacks or if you lose the body-to-subframe alignment for some reason, it can be restored. Adjacent to the center mount flange on the subframe (rearward of the front wheelwells) is an alignment hole that pilots to a similar hole in the unitized body. Use a simple

1/2" socket extension or two-inch-long 5/8" OD dowel through these holes to regain alignment.

On severely rusty cars, there may be little body left to attach the subframe mounts to. The rear four mounts bolt into cage nuts tack-welded to the car floorpan. These cage nuts are not available separately—a junkyard is your only source. If the subframe pads themselves are rusted, precut patch panels are available from Camaro mail-order houses for about $50. These must be welded in.

You can buy a set of six replacement mounts from Camaro mail-order parts outlets. If the original bolts

and washers are corroded, missing or damaged, replace them as well. The mounts vary somewhat in size over the years so make sure you specify what year your Camaro is.

Also the mounts may be of different sizes, so take care to match up what goes where. On 1967–69 models, the radiator-support mounts are 2-1/2 x 9/16", the middle mounts are 2-1/2 x 7/8" and the rears measure 2-1/8" around.

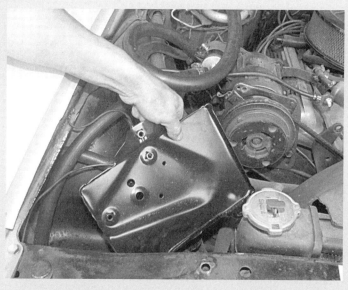

2. To gain access to the radiator-support-to-subframe mounts, remove the fender-to-radiator-support braces, the battery, and tray, as well as the windshield-washer reservoir.

3. Pick which side you'll do first and start unbolting the mounts on that side. Leave the other side alone to keep the alignment for now. Most can use a good shot of penetrating oil. On the front mounts, block the bolt from turning and remove the nut from the bottom.

4. Fish out the bolt for the front mount from the top.

5. If your Camaro's rocker panels aren't rusty, place a stout wood block on a floor jack and lift the car an inch or so on one side via the rocker-panel-to-floorpan weld flange. Position the block as shown, perpendicular to the front of the door opening. This allows you to remove the upper halves of the two rear mounts.

6. Unbolt the two rear mounts on one side. This rear mount had almost disintegrated over time.

7. Remove the upper half of the mounts. This one came out easily, but some will have to be pried out.

8. Access to the half of the front mounts between the subframe and radiator support can be gained through the wheel openings, as Bob Cox of Camaros Only demonstrates.

9. Old, dried-up mount (left) was deformed and compressed. New mount (right) will help absorb road noise and driveline vibration.

10. New mount set from Year One, Inc. along with new hardware is laid out for installation. Each pair of mounts (front, middle and rear) is different, so don't get them mixed up.

11. If your mount hardware is rusty or chewed up, it's a good idea to use new hardware. If you're concerned about appearance, try bead-blasting the factory bolts and washers, then painting them with a semi-flat black. Or you can order new hardware that maintains the correct factory appearance but costs twice as much as the generic stuff.

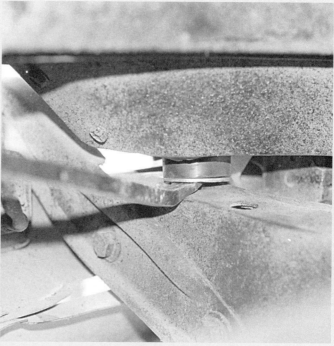

12. Bob installs new rear mounts. Snug these down for now. When the car is on the ground, these will be torqued to 75-95 ft-lb.

13. Some mounts need to be coaxed into position.

14. The center mounts have alignment holes to index the subframe with the body.

15. The most stubborn mount will likely be the front one under the battery. Years of battery-acid-induced corrosion make this a tough one.

16. With fresh subframe mounts installed, your Camaro should ride more like General Motors intended.

Chapter 27

Front-End Rebuild

1. In for a dime, in for a dollar. Once you start tearing things apart, you might as well replace all front-end parts that will eventually wear out. This kit from PST Engineering includes upper and lower ball joints, upper and lower control arm pivot bushings, upper control arm pivot shafts, anti-roll bar pivots, bushings and links, inner and outer tie-rod ends, tie-rod sleeves and clamps, rubber snubbers, idler arm and all necessary grease fittings, rubber boots, cotter pins and attaching hardware. To this list, you may want to add a set of front springs and a Pitman arm.

The double A-arm front suspension and recirculating-ball steering with parallelogram linkage used in all 1967–81 Camaros are sturdy, easy to service, and given normal care, wear, and tear, should last a lifetime. Aside from obvious care taken to avoid huge bumps, potholes and other serious shocks to the front end, the trick to achieving longevity is keeping the ball joints and steering linkage lubed. That said, time is rubber's great enemy and even on pampered Camaros, the control-arm bushings will deteriorate and affect wheel alignment, and the boots on the ball joints and steering linkage will crack and tear, allowing dirt and moisture into the joints.

I could present a complete chapter just on front-end troubleshooting. But basically it boils down to two things: How does the car feel going down the road and what does front tire wear look like? If there's no play in the steering, no shake, clunks or groans when you hit a bump or turn the wheel and the tires have even wear, chances are you can postpone a front-end redo. But you might consider having an alignment specialist look at your Camaro and set camber, caster and toe-in to factory specs. If anything's seriously worn out, he'll notice it right away.

On the other hand, on a decades-old Camaro, odds are several of the front end's numerous wear points have reached critical mass. Whereas you can inspect and replace a ball joint here and a tie-rod end there, the most cost-effective way to approach a front-end job is to replace everything. The biggest expense and hassle is wrestling everything apart and piecing it back together. If you can't do the work yourself, count on spending several hundred dollars in shop labor and machine-shop fees. Replacement parts for vintage Camaros

---

Tools & Supplies Needed
- Spring compressor
- Pickle fork
- Jack stands
- Floor jack
- Hammer
- Needle-nose pliers
- Socket set (1/2" drive)
- Open-end wrench set
- Bailing wire (or coat hanger)
- White grease
- WD40 penetrant or equivalent
- Eastwood Chassis Black paint or equivalent
- Eastwood Spray Gray paint or equivalent
- E-Z Off oven cleaner or equivalent
- Sandblaster
- Tape measure
- Grease gun
- Silicone spray

---

are not exorbitantly expensive. For example, the Performance Suspension Technology front-end kit we installed in our '67 Rally Sport project car was reasonably priced. Plan on more money to replace a pair of sagging front springs. Shock absorbers can be replaced at any time. To get the expert touch that only comes with experience, we took our RS to Bob Cox of Camaros Only in Brea, California.

To do the job yourself, you'll need a spring compressor, a pickle fork, some sturdy jack stands and pneumatic tools if possible. Most people will have to farm out the job of pressing out (and in) the control-arm bushings and ball joints to a machine shop. If this is a car you plan to keep and possibly show, take this opportunity to detail the front end as it's disassembled. Necessary steps include degreasing, sandblasting and painting the control arms. You can also detail the upper-arm pivot shafts, ball joints and steering-linkage components with a spray coating that looks like unpainted steel. This paint then has to dry before it can be handled. So timing is critical. If you're doing this over a weekend, get the front end taken apart on a Friday night. Take the control arms to the machine shop on Saturday morning to get the bushings and ball joints pressed out. Then degrease, sandblast and paint the control arms and have the ball joints and bushings pressed in later that afternoon.

I can't emphasize safety enough when working on the front end. First off, support the car securely on jack stands. Never venture underneath with the car raised only on a bumper jack or even a floor jack. Second, wear safety glasses to keep out of your eyes dirt, rust, grease and other debris that will rain down on you as you disassemble the front end. Third, the front springs are retained under great pressure. Should a coil spring pop loose while you are working on the lower control arms, it could seriously injure you. Always use a sturdy spring

compressor and exercise great care around the springs. Never put fingers in a position where they could be crushed if some component suddenly shifted position or came loose.

When you're working under the front end, a big pain is the crud, clumps of caked-on oily dirt, grease, rust—all of it overhead. You'll knock it loose getting things apart, then lay in it as the project progresses. I recommend getting a large cardboard box (for an appliance, a computer or something), cutting it open and spreading it out as sort of a combination catchpan for crud and pad to lie and slide around on under there. Periodically, pull it out and dump the accumulated crud into the trash can. This makes for a cleaner, much more pleasurable environment to work in.

The only major difference between the first- and second-generation cars is the location of the steering linkage—behind the axle centerline on 1967–69 models and ahead of the axle on 1970–81s.

Line up an alignment shop where you'll take your car to after replacing the front-end components. Even though you may carefully replicate the tie-rod settings and upper-control-arm shim configurations, the alignment could be seriously out of spec—and this could affect the dynamic handling qualities of the car. Now let's get busy.

2. After loosening the lugnuts for the front wheels, jack up the car about two feet and support under the front subframe as shown with a pair of sturdy jack stands. Then remove the front wheels.

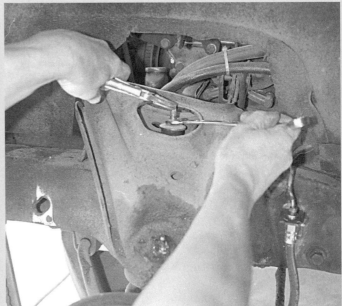

3. First out are the shock absorbers. With pliers or a small open-end wrench, hold the top of the shock shaft from turning while you remove the nuts for the upper mount.

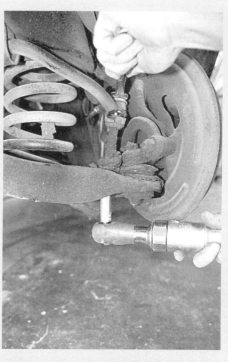

5. Unbolt the anti-roll bar links from the lower control arms. Hold the nuts from turning with a wrench while removing the long link bolts. Discard the old rubber bushings, which, as you can see, had deteriorated badly.

4. Remove the two hex screws for the lower shock mount and slide the shock out through the lower control arm.

6. With a screwdriver, scrape away accumulated grease and dirt from around the upper and lower ball-joint stud nuts and tie-rod end nuts. Then pull out the cotter pins for these nuts with needle-nose pliers or wire cutters.

7. Remove the nut for each outer tie-rod end and separate the tie rod from the steering knuckle using a pickle fork and hammer.

8. Support the lower control arm with a floor jack. Unbolt the large castellated hex nut from the lower ball joint.

9. Lower the floor jack about an inch under the lower control arm. Being careful to stay clear of the lower control arm, use a pickle fork and hammer to separate the lower ball joint and knuckle from the control arm. It will pop free with great force because the coil spring is trying to expand to its unloaded length!

10. With your foot, push down on the lower control arm until the coil spring pops out.

11. Loosen the castellated nut on the upper ball-joint stud until only three or four threads retain it to the stud. Then use a pickle fork and hammer to separate the upper ball joint and knuckle from its control arm. Leaving the stud nut partially on prevents damaging the flexible brake hose due to the weight of the knuckle and brake unit hanging from it.

12. Tie the knuckle to the subframe or flexible brake hose bracket to support it. Then remove the upper ball joint stud nut. Leaving the brake hoses connected eliminates having to bleed the hydraulic system later on. Repeat for the other side.

13. If you're replacing coil springs, check the new against the old. Make sure the coil diameter, number of coils and spring length are the same. Springs vary greatly year to year and model to model. For instance, these 1967 small-block springs for a car with air conditioning were longer than those for a car without.

14. Spray with penetrating oil and unbolt the lower control arms from the subframe. Sometimes these bolts rust in position, so be patient.

15. Make sure the steering wheel and front wheel are pointed straight ahead before removing any steering linkage. Remove the nut for the Pitman arm. You'll need a special puller to separate the Pitman arm from the steering box.

16. Unbolt the idler arm from the subframe. You can replace steering-linkage components piecemeal, but since we're renewing the whole front end, it's easier to drop the linkage as a unit and disassemble it on the bench.

17. Steering linkage ready for disassembly. We're going to replace everything but the center link (which has no moving parts). Don't disturb the adjustments of the tie rods by loosening their sleeves. You'll need this information later on when adjusting the new tie rods to the same length as the old, thus preserving the toe-in adjustment as much as possible.

18. Remove the cotter pins and castellated nuts retaining the inner tie-rod ends to the center link. Separate them using a hammer and pickle fork.

19. Next out are the upper control arms. First count the number, thickness and placement of shims (arrows) between each upper control arm pivot shaft and the subframe. Bob Cox of Camaros Only recommends wrapping the shim stacks in masking tape and labeling them as to location. The shims are used to adjust caster and camber.

20. Remove the two nuts for each upper control arm pivot shaft.

21. Using a pry bar or long, stout screwdriver, lever the upper control arm off the subframe studs.

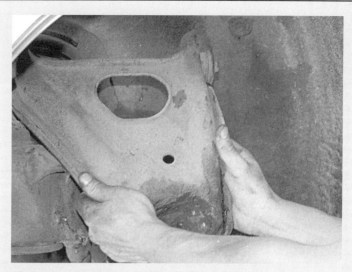

22. Remove the upper control arm. Repeat for other side.

23. Spray the control arms and center link with oven cleaner and place in the sun to remove grease buildup. After an hour or so, hose off with high-pressure water.

24. The arena now shifts to the control arms, which must be stripped of their old ball joints and pivot bushings. You may elect to have this done at a machine shop. Special tools are required. But if you have access to the lower ball-joint puller and pneumatic tools, it can be done on the bench as Bob Cox from Camaros Only will demonstrate. To remove the lower ball joint, use a large clamp, which supports the control arm, and the joint is driven out by large screw acting on ball stud.

25. Original upper ball joints are riveted to control arms. Simply cut off rivet heads with a chisel.

26. Then tap out rivets with a punch and upper ball joint lifts right out.

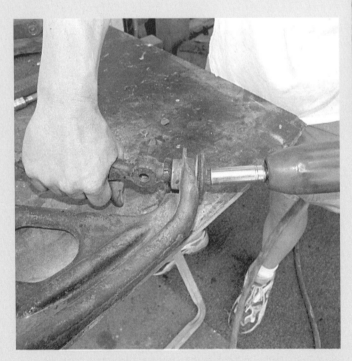

27. Remove the nuts and large washers from the ends of the upper control arm pivot shaft.

28. Hit the control arm bushings with some penetrating oil to ease their removal. Then drive out the bushings with an air chisel. Use care not to gouge or otherwise damage the control arms in the process. Alternatively, you can have the bushings pressed out at a machine shop. Repeat for the other upper control arm and both lower control arms.

29. If you have the time and facilities available, by all means sandblast the stripped control arms. A detailed front end separates the poseurs from the players at car shows. Here, Bob Cox of Camaros Only places an upper control arm into the sandblasting booth.

30. After sandblasting, give the arms a heavy coat of Eastwood Chassis Black. This enamel has high solids and excellent chip resistance. Give it at least two hours to dry—overnight is best.

31. The ball joints, pivot shafts, tie rods, idler and Pitman arms can be painted with Eastwood Spray Gray. This duplicates the original unpainted steel look and prevents them from rusting. Be careful to mask off the threads and machined areas when painting.

32. For greater long-term durability, you can try these PST polygraphite bushings, which won't crack and decompose like stock rubber bushings. Transmitted road noise may increase slightly, but handling will improve because the polygraphite bushings deflect less under load. For best success and squeak-free operation, apply silicone grease included in kit to all friction surfaces.

33. Lube the OD of the new bushings with WD40 or equivalent.

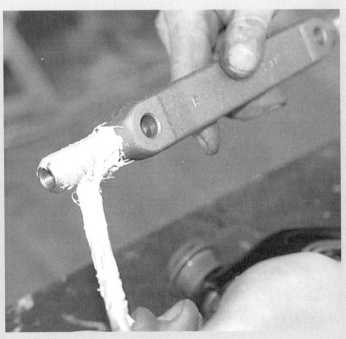

34. Coat the machined ends of the upper control arm pivot shafts with white grease. This keeps them from seizing in the bushing bores.

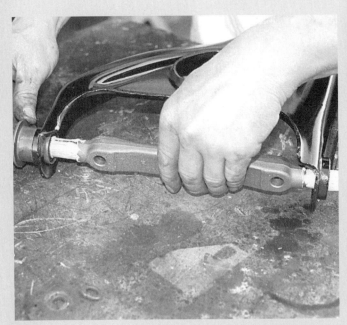

35. Assemble the upper arms first. Slide in one bushing by hand, slip in the pivot shaft and slide in the opposite bushing by hand. Note that bushings slide in from outboard ends toward middle.

36. Without use of a press, you can finesse the control arm bushings into place using a pneumatic driver and a drift. The trick is to work around the collar of the bushing with the driver, taking care not to deform it.

37. Alternately, put the large washers and nuts on the ends of the pivot shafts and pull the new bushings into position using the threaded shafts.

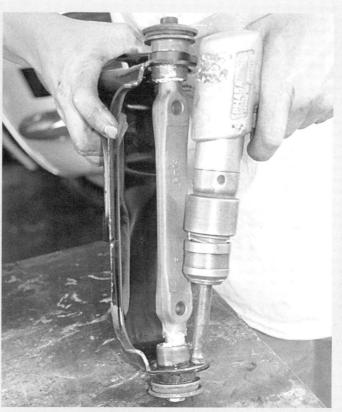

38. Occasionally, the bushings will bind in the arm, bowing it inward. To relieve this bind, push the wall of the arm in the opposite direction with the pneumatic driver. Tighten the upper arm cap bolts to 45 ft-lb. Repeat for the other arm.

39. Slide the upper ball joint into the upper control arm, slip on rubber boot and metal sleeve. Apply Loctite to the four ball joint retaining bolts (that replace the previous rivets), install the bolts and tighten the nuts to 20-25 ft-lb. Tip: To keep nuts from turning, hold them with an open-end wrench turned sideways. Repeat for the other arm.

40. Install the upper ball joint grease fittings.

42. Install the pivot bushings into the lower arms in the same way you did the uppers, except here there are no pivot shafts.

41. Place the assembled upper arm onto the subframe studs, using the same amount of shims in the same locations as before. Tighten the retaining nuts to 50 ft-lb.

43. The lower ball joint is pressed into position. Here, Bob Cox of Camaros Only uses this stout clamp with a pneumatic ram. Don't install the lower ball joint grease fittings just yet.

44. Coat the lower control arm pivot bolts with white grease to prevent them from binding or rusting in the bushings if the car sits for a long time under humid conditions.

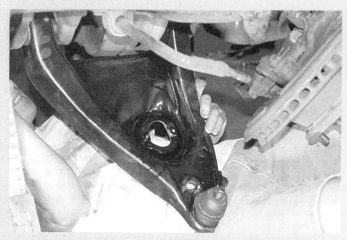

45. Install the lower arms to the subframe. Slide the bolts in from the front and tighten the bolts to 50 ft-lb.

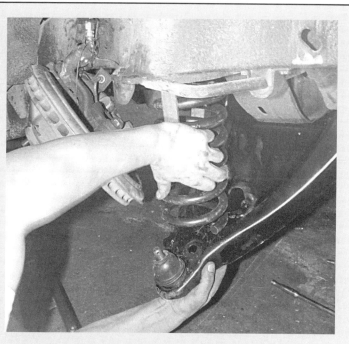

46. Here's where it pays to eat your Wheaties for breakfast. You'll need a spring compressor capable of compressing the coil springs at least 2-1/2" to be able to get them into position. Be very careful. If a spring should slip out of the compressor and hit you, it could result in serious injury. New coil springs are just a shade longer than the tired, saggy springs they replace, making installation all the more difficult. If you don't know what you are doing, or don't have the right tools, don't try this procedure! Now compress the spring with the tool and raise it up into the spring cavity in the subframe. Push the bottom of the spring over the shock-absorber hole with your foot. Hold the spring in place with the lower control arm.

47. Using a floor jack and a protective wood block, raise the lower control arm until just before the car starts to lift off the jack stand. Make sure the ends of the coils are indexed in their pockets. Turn the spring, if necessary, with a large screwdriver. Then release the spring compressor.

48. While supporting the knuckle and brake unit, cut the bailing wire and seat the knuckle on the lower ball joint. Install the nut, tighten to 65 ft-lb and install the cotter pin.

49. Then push down on the upper control arm and connect the upper ball joint to the knuckle. Coax into position with a hammer. Install the nut, tighten to 50-ft lb and install the cotter pin. Lower the floor jack. Install the lower ball joint grease fitting. Repeat for the other side. Reinstall the shock absorbers.

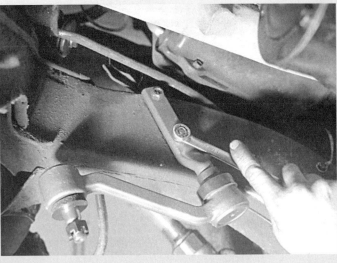

50. Install the idler arm to the subframe. Tighten the two nuts to 40 ft-lb.

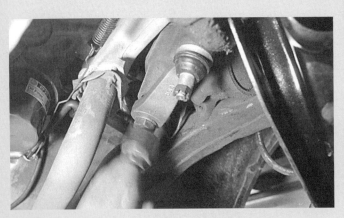

51. Install the Pitman arm on the steering shaft. Tighten the nut to 140 ft-lb.

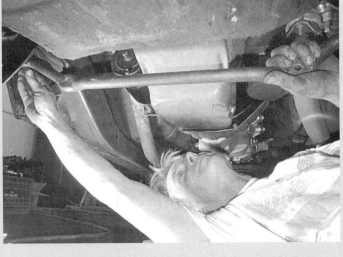

52. Offer up the center link and connect it to the idler and Pitman arms. Tighten the nuts to 35 ft-lb and install new cotter pins.

53. Measure the length of the old tie rods, center to center, one side at a time. Adjust the new tie rods to the same length. Do so by loosening the clamp bolts and rotating the sleeves, not the ends.

54. When each tie rod is adjusted to the correct length, tighten the clamp nuts to 130 in-lb.

55. Install the tie rods. Tighten the nuts to 35 ft lb and install new cotter pins.

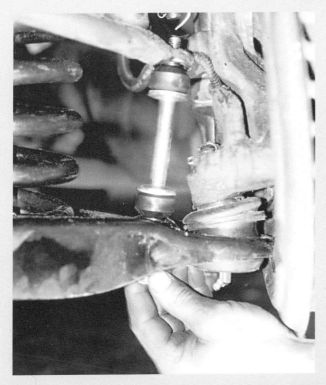

56. Install new anti-roll bar bushings, links and washers. Tighten the link bolts to 8 ft-lb.

57. With the front end gone through, expect shimmy-free and clunk-free driving as well as precise handling for years to come.

ABOUT THE AUTHOR

Ron Sessions has been writing about cars since 1971 when he joined the Chilton Book Company to work on auto repair manuals for the do-it-yourselfer. A half decade later, Ron was scripting new-product training videos for one of Chevrolet's largest agencies, the Sandy Corporation. During a seven-year editorial stint with the automotive-enthusiast publisher HPBooks, Ron wrote his first book, *Turbo Hydra-Matic 350 Handbook.* In 1987, Ron became editor of *Road & Track Specials* publications, such as the annual *Car Buyer's Guide.* He created *Exotic Cars Quarterly* magazine, as well as the high-quality 4WD adventure magazine, *Open Road.* Between issues, Ron found time to author three more books, *How to Work with and Modify the Turbo Hydra-Matic 400 Transmission, Camaro Restoration Handbook,* and *Camaro Owner's Handbook.*

In 2002, Ron moved to *Motor Trend* magazine as senior editor. Also breaking cover that year was *Lust, Then Love,* Ron's coffee table book on Nissan's new 350Z.

Over the years, Ron has written hundreds of articles and had thousands of photos published on automotive subjects. His byline and/or photo credits have appeared in *All Chevy, Auto, Auto Hebdo, Automobile, Bilsport, Camaro/Trans Am, Car Craft, Chevy High Performance, Corvette Illustrated, Four Wheeler, Gear, GMBuyPower.com, Motor of Japan, Musclecar Review, Mustang Monthly, Popular Mechanics, Popular Science, Sport Auto, Super Ford, Travel Holiday, Truck Trend* and *Viper Quarterly.* He also contributed on automotive subjects for the *Houston Chronicle,* *OC Metro,* and the *Cleveland Plain Dealer.*

In 2005, at the request of then–General Motors vice chairman Bob Lutz, Ron joined a small group of seasoned car magazine editors and road testers to advise the company on the design, engineering, and development of new products. These included the all-new fifth generation Camaro, 2008 Cadillac CTS and CTS-V, 2010 Buick Regal, and Chevrolet Volt, among others.

HPBooks

GENERAL MOTORS
Big-Block Chevy Engine Buildups: 978-1-55788-484-8/HP1484
Big-Block Chevy Performance: 978-1-55788-216-5/HP1216
Building the Chevy LS Engine: 978-1-55788-559-3/HP1559
Camaro Performance Handbook: 978-1-55788-057-4/HP1057
Camaro Restoration Handbook ('61–'81): 978-0-89586-375-1/HP758
Chevy LS Engine Buildups: 978-1-55788-567-8/HP1567
Chevy LS Engine Conversion Handbook: 978-1-55788-566-1/HP1566
Chevy LS1/LS6 Performance: 978-1-55788-407-7/HP1407
Classic Camaro Restoration, Repair & Upgrades:
  978-1-55788-564-7/HP1564
The Classic Chevy Truck Handbook: 978-1-55788-534-0/HP1534
How to Rebuild Big-Block Chevy Engines:
  978-0-89586-175-7/HP755
How to Rebuild Big-Block Chevy Engines, 1991–2000:
  978-1-55788-550-0/HP1550
How to Rebuild Small-Block Chevy LT-1/LT-4 Engines:
  978-1-55788-393-3/HP1393
How to Rebuild Your Small-Block Chevy:
  978-1-55788-029-1/HP1029
Powerglide Transmission Handbook: 978-1-55788-355-1/HP1355
Small-Block Chevy Engine Buildups: 978-1-55788-400-8/HP1400
Turbo Hydra-Matic 350 Handbook: 978-0-89586-051-4/HP511

FORD
Classic Mustang Restoration, Repair & Upgrades:
  978-1-55788-537-1/HP1537
Ford Engine Buildups: 978-1-55788-531-9/HP1531
Ford Windsor Small-Block Performance:
  978-1-55788-558-6/HP1558
How to Build Small-Block Ford Racing Engines:
  978-1-55788-536-2/HP1536
How to Rebuild Big-Block Ford Engines:
  978-0-89586-070-5/HP708
How to Rebuild Ford V-8 Engines: 978-0-89586-036-1/HP36
How to Rebuild Small-Block Ford Engines:
  978-0-912656-89-2/HP89
Mustang Restoration Handbook: 978-0-89586-402-4/HP029

MOPAR
Big-Block Mopar Performance: 978-1-55788-302-5/HP1302
How to Hot Rod Small-Block Mopar Engine, Revised:
  978-1-55788-405-3/HP1405
How to Modify Your Jeep Chassis and Suspension For Off-Road:
  978-1-55788-424-4/HP1424
How to Modify Your Mopar Magnum V8:
  978-1-55788-473-2/HP1473
How to Rebuild and Modify Chrysler 426 Hemi Engines:
  978-1-55788-525-8/HP1525
How to Rebuild Big-Block Mopar Engines:
  978-1-55788-190-8/HP1190
How to Rebuild Small-Block Mopar Engines:
  978-0-89586-128-5/HP83
How to Rebuild Your Mopar Magnum V8:
  978-1-55788-431-5/HP1431
The Mopar Six-Pack Engine Handbook:
  978-1-55788-528-9/HP1528
Torqueflite A-727 Transmission Handbook:
  978-1-55788-399-5/HP1399

IMPORTS
Baja Bugs & Buggies: 978-0-89586-186-3/HP60
Honda/Acura Engine Performance: 978-1-55788-384-1/HP1384
How to Build Performance Nissan Sport Compacts, 1991–2006:
  978-1-55788-541-8/HP1541

How to Hot Rod VW Engines: 978-0-91265-603-8/HP034
How to Rebuild Your VW Air-Cooled Engine:
  978-0-89586-225-9/HP1225
Porsche 911 Performance: 978-1-55788-489-3/HP1489
Street Rotary: 978-1-55788-549-4/HP1549
Toyota MR2 Performance: 978-155788-553-1/HP1553
Xtreme Honda B-Series Engines: 978-1-55788-552-4/HP1552

HANDBOOKS
Auto Electrical Handbook: 978-0-89586-238-9/HP387
Auto Math Handbook: 978-1-55788-020-8/HP1020
Auto Upholstery & Interiors: 978-1-55788-265-3/HP1265
Custom Auto Wiring & Electrical: 978-1-55788-545-6/HP1545
Electric Vehicle Conversion Handbook: 978-1-55788-568-5/HP1568
Engine Builder's Handbook: 978-1-55788-245-5/HP1245
Fiberglass & Other Composite Materials: 978-1-55788-498-
  5/HP1498
High Performance Fasteners & Plumbing: 978-1-55788-523-
  4/HP1523
Metal Fabricator's Handbook: 978-0-89586-870-1/HP709
Paint & Body Handbook: 978-1-55788-082-6/HP1082
Practical Auto & Truck Restoration: 978-155788-547-0/HP1547
Pro Paint & Body: 978-1-55788-394-0/HP1394
Sheet Metal Handbook: 978-0-89586-757-5/HP575
Welder's Handbook, Revised: 978-1-55788-513-5

INDUCTION
Engine Airflow, 978-155788-537-1/HP1537
Holley 4150 & 4160 Carburetor Handbook: 978-0-89586-047-
  7/HP473
Holley Carbs, Manifolds & F.I.: 978-1-55788-052-9/HP1052
Rebuild & Powertune Carter/Edelbrock Carburetors:
  978-155788-555-5/HP1555
Rochester Carburetors: 978-0-89586-301-0/HP014
Performance Fuel Injection Systems: 978-1-55788-557-9/HP1557
Turbochargers: 978-0-89586-135-1/HP49
Street Turbocharging: 978-1-55788-488-6/HP1488
Weber Carburetors: 978-0-89589-377-5/HP774

RACING & CHASSIS
Advanced Race Car Chassis Technology: 978-1-55788-562-3/HP562
Chassis Engineering: 978-1-55788-055-0/HP1055
4Wheel & Off-Road's Chassis & Suspension: 978-1-55788-406-
  0/HP1406
How to Make Your Car Handle: 978-1-91265-646-5/HP46
How to Build a Winning Drag Race Chassis & Suspension:
The Race Car Chassis: 978-1-55788-540-1/HP1540
The Racing Engine Builder's Handbook: 978-1-55788-492-3/HP1492

STREET RODS
Street Rodder magazine's Chassis & Suspension Handbook: 978-
  1-55788-346-9/HP1346
Street Rodder's Handbook, Revised: 978-1-55788-409-1/HP1409

ORDER YOUR COPY TODAY!
All books are available from online bookstores
(www.amazon.com and www.barnesandnoble.com) and auto
parts stores (www.summitracing.com or www.jegs.com). Or
order direct from HPBooks at www.penguin.com/hpauto. Many
titles are available in downloadable eBook formats.

170